THE ESSENTIAL CYCLIST

Other books by the author:

Bicycling Medicine

Essentials of Bicycle Racing and Training

Smart Cycling

THE ESSENTIAL CYCLIST

ARNIE BAKER, M.D.

THE LYONS PRESS

Printed in the United States of America

Designed by Joel Friedlander, Marin Bookworks, San Rafael, CA

Illustrations by Mitchell Heinze

10 9 8 7 6 5 4 3 2 1

Library of Congress Cataloging-in-Publication Data
Baker, Arnie.
    The essential cyclist / Arnie Baker.
        p. cm.
    Includes bibliographical references and index.
    ISBN 1-55821-522-0 (pbk.)
    1. Cycling   2. Cycling—Equipment and supplies.   3. Cycling—Safety measures.   I. Title
GV1041.B24   1998
796.6—dc21   97-44824
                                                            CIP

Dedicated to the Leukemia Society of America's Team in Training—an endurance program that promotes bicycling for riders novice to expert, while raising funds to help find a cure for leukemia and its related cancers.

CONTENTS

ACKNOWLEDGMENTS

I have been helped by many, not only in the specific preparation of this book, but also in my development as a coach and as a racer.

I'd like to specifically thank Barbara Baker and Brian Begley, for help and suggestions with the early manuscript; Steve Jonas, whose suggestion helped bring about this book; Lilly Golden, my editor at the Lyons Press; and Gero McGuffin, who has not only helped in editing and criticism but who also rides with me every day.

FOREWORD

I have been very fortunate in being able to make my living from bicycling for more than twenty years, first as a BMX racer and then as a professional mountain biker. However, bicycling is not just the way I earn a living. As a bicycle rider, I have had years of enjoyment with plenty of exercise and travel; perhaps best of all, I have met many wonderful people throughout the United States and all over the world.

In fact, with Arnie's help as my coach, I am still, after all these years, learning more about the sport of bicycle racing.

Perhaps you have just started bicycling, have just bought your first bicycle, or perhaps your old bike is just sitting collecting dust in your garage.

Don't miss the opportunity to get some great exercise, have fun, and meet new people. Read Arnie's book and get that bicycle out. I wish you all the best and who knows: maybe I'll see you on the road or on the trail—be sure to wave!

—Tinker Juarez, Olympian and multiple national
mountain biking champion, spring 1998

WHY RIDE A BIKE?

Why ride? I mean it. There are so many things to do, how can you take the time to ride a bike? If you're not a rider, it's easy to dismiss cycling as something just for kids. But there are so many good reasons to ride a bike, the real question is: How can you afford not to?

PHYSICAL HEALTH

The perception that bicycle riding is good for your health is an important reason why many adult Americans ride. And it's more than just a perception—it's a fact.

Many people use cycling as part of a program to control weight, blood pressure, or cholesterol. Cycling helps improve agility, balance, and reaction time. And it's not as hard on the joints as are many other forms of exercise, such as running.

Cycling is useful not only in promoting good health and preventing illness but also in rehabilitation. For example, it can be an important part of rehabilitation from knee surgery.

Many people feel that cycling helps them be healthier and live longer. Margaret Nolan is sixty-seven years old. She purchased her first bike for fun and fitness five years ago. A friend encouraged her to join his bicycle club, a master's racing club. Racing was the furthest thing from her mind, but not long ago she learned about the California Senior Olympics and decided to enter three races. There were no other competitors in her field—she won three gold medals.

She found a group to ride with regularly and to train with for time trials—solo races over a prescribed distance for time. Margaret Nolan became an athlete. At the time trials she was the oldest woman in her group. Individual effort was rewarded, not absolute time. After three years of riding a bicycle, initially competing against only herself, she discovered national competition and became a U.S. national champion in her time-trial events. She then teamed up with a "younger man" to ride a tandem—for a combined age of 110 years. How fast could Margaret go? She rode roughly 25 miles in roughly 55 minutes, to set another U.S. record.

PSYCHOLOGICAL HEALTH

Cycling can be a great stress reducer. Riding slowly is relaxing. Sometimes it's great to commute to and from work at 8 miles an hour. I look at the flowers, enjoy the great view of the city and San Diego bay, and relax. Going fast relaxes me, too. I feel physically spent and mentally at ease after I've raced and exerted myself at 30 miles per hour. Cycling inspires confidence, clears the head of anxiety, and gives the rider time to think.

Riding up Mt. Palomar, in Southern California, my riding buddies and I often meet up with a guy named Dale. We don't know his last name. Most riders are intimidated by the 4,000-foot climb. On his heavy mountain bike, Dale passes most of us on the way up. Dale has just one leg, and he rides without a prosthesis.

ENVIRONMENTALLY SENSIBLE TRANSPORTATION

Let's face it. We use our cars a lot. How many of us get in our cars to pick up a quart of milk two blocks away? Or use our cars to commute a few miles to work? But cars are polluting. Bicycles are responsible for some pollution, of course, in their manufacture and in their use of tires and tubes that need to be replaced. But per mile, there's no other mode of transportation (other than walking) that is as environmentally friendly.

The bike, in fact, is the most efficient of all forms of transportation. For journeys of up to 5 miles, it is often just as fast to bicycle as it is to take the bus or drive. And it's even possible for the bicycle to transport nearly a ton of material on its frame. I'm not suggesting that for your fragile, lightweight racing bike, but many people do use a bike to carry groceries or to transport other goods.

SOCIALIZING

Sure, it's obvious: Go to a singles bike club alone on a tandem and you might find companionship. But the social aspects of riding can be much more than that. Cycling clubs provide a local network, as do organized tours. Bicycling is often the tie that binds picnicking, visiting restaurants, camping, and other activities.

Of course, you don't need to join a club. Whereas cars enclose their drivers and create an insular environment, bikes do just the opposite. Riding with a few friends is great. Even riding alone and waving to or meeting other riders is a great interaction.

TOURING

Whether it's around the block or across the country, a bicycle lets you see the sights. Running doesn't allow you to cover much ground, and cars go so fast that you miss a lot when touring. Bicycling, you might cover 15 miles in an hour's ride. That's a lot of territory. You can ride to a park or to the next town, check out that new housing development, or go on a pastry-shop crawl.

If you are touring, you can spend a month seeing most of a good section of the Atlantic or Pacific coast. Or the Rockies. Or a few European countries. Every year my wife and I take a two-week touring trip and as many long weekends as we can—a great way to get some exercise and see the scenery, eat a lot (my wife considers ice cream and pie to be important food groups), and just relax. Whether it's looking at the flowers or serious tourism, a bicycle can be the best vehicle.

FAMILY

From the parent teaching the child how to ride to going out as a family for a Sunday spin, from short trips with bike trailers for small children to child conversion kits on tandems to cycling vacations: Cycling is good for the whole family. Imagine your bike so intertwined with your life that you ride 350 miles every week for decades, not including weekends. Imagine having a child who reaches the age of fifteen before she realizes that a vacation can mean something other than two or three weeks of daily double, triple, and quadruple centuries (100-mile races)—or crossing the continent. That's how it is for Pete Penseyres's family.

Pete's license plate says RAAM (for the Race Across America, an annual race from the Pacific to the Atlantic). Pete and his bike have covered more ground and made more transcontinental crossings than most of us will ever record in our cars. Quiet, determined, and calculating, Pete has spent his life figuring out how to get the most miles and fun out of his bike. Much of his success is attributable to his wife, Joanne, who is the real organizer in the family.

Although Pete gets most of the press, his brother Jim is perhaps more inspirational. Jim races with a prosthesis (he lost part of a leg as a result of a war injury in Vietnam). Jim has completed three solo RAAMs, also with the active support of his family.

COMPETITION

Whether you're interested in improving your own performance up that climb, besting a friend, or going to the Olympics, cycling can be a great competitive outlet. Almost all towns and cities have competitive cycling groups or licensed racing clubs. Go to your local bicycle store for information and help in finding these groups.

Competitions exist for many forms of bicycling. There are BMX races (mostly for kids and youths) and competitions for mountain bikes, road bikes, track bikes, and human-powered vehicles. Competition may be strictly local or international.

Although most people in the United States think that football, baseball, and basketball are the great sports, from the global perspective it's cycling.

More than fifteen million people attend the Tour de France, a multiday bike race held in France each July.

CHARITY

A number of charities hold bicycling events or rides to help raise money. The Leukemia Society of America has gone one step further and provides months of training and support to help individuals raise money and successfully complete a 100-mile ride.

Linda Sorkin had leukemia. She joined the Leukemia Society's Team in Training to help raise money to find a cure for the disease by riding a century—100 miles. She started out training only a few months ago. She may not be very fast yet, but she's committed and she's steady. Just recently we rode 75 miles together.

GOOD FOR BUSINESS

Bicycle messengers are an important feature of the urban office environment. Although bicycle grocery delivery is disappearing, bicycle delivery is still an employment option. And you've heard of the power lunch? Or golfing as a rite of passage with business associates? For some people, bicycling is great networking. In my community, a lot of important business takes place on bicycles.

FASHION

Fashion is important to some of us. And cycling is an excuse to buy splashy jerseys, tight shorts, and other accessories. Cycling fashion is so in vogue that many people who don't cycle wear cycling clothes!

VANITY

Let's face it. Exercise helps you look better. It gives color to the cheeks, tone to the muscles, and it reduces flab. Of course, you don't only look better, you are healthier, too.

IT'S INEXPENSIVE

You can buy a bicycle for a couple of hundred dollars. Actually, you can be lucky and find a good used bicycle for less at a garage sale or through a classified ad. Although an inexpensive bike can be purchased at department stores, the professional assembly and higher quality of a bicycle obtained from a specialty bicycle store is usually worth the price.

You can spend thousands of dollars on a bicycle—just as you can spend tens of thousands of dollars on a car.

EAT MORE

Ride more, burn more calories. If you ride enough, you need to eat more. For those of us who like to eat, it's a great deal.

FUN

There are many reasons to ride. Perhaps the best one is that it's fun. There aren't many things that are good for you and fun, too.

EQUIPMENT

TYPES OF BIKES

There are many types of bicycles, suitable for different types of riding. Here are the most commonly available types:

ROAD (RACING) BIKES

Uses: Road bikes are used for racing, performance, and fitness riding on paved roads. Riders are in an aerodynamic, bent-over position. Road bikes offer the least rolling resistance.

Frame: Shorter wheelbase than touring bicycles, with steeper seat and head tubes and less clearance between pedals and front wheel. This gives a quick, responsive ride—a ride some find "twitchy" or stiff compared with that of touring bikes, especially on rough surfaces. Double-butted steel,* aluminum, titanium, or carbon-fiber tubing.

Gears: Two chain rings. 14–18 gears. Narrow range. Index shifting.

Wheels: 700c (metric size, a little less than 27"). Occasionally, 26".

Tires: High-pressure, very narrow—less than 23 mm wide. These reduce rolling resistance but are unsuitable for loose surfaces.

Handlebars: Drop style. Give a choice of hand positions, important in allowing the rider to get into a "tuck," a bent-over, aerodynamic position.

Brakes: Side- or center-pull.

Saddle: Narrow, often hard.

Pedals: Clipless.

Weight: Under 22 pounds.

TRIATHLON (RACING) BIKES

---

*A note on tubing: Steel, the traditional choice of frame building, is relatively heavy when compared with more modern aluminum, titanium, or carbon fiber. Most mechanical stresses occur at the ends of bicycle tubes. The center sections of tube can be thinner, leaving thicker, or butted, ends. If both ends are thicker, they are said to be double-butted.

Uses: Triathlon bikes are used on the cycling time-trial leg of triathlons.

Frame: A steeply angled seat tube allows a more forward saddle position. Double-butted steel, aluminum, titanium, or carbon-fiber tubing.

Gears: Two chain rings. 14–18 gears. Narrow range. Index shifting.

Wheels: 700c or 26". A lightly spoked front wheel and a similar or disc rear wheel are used to reduce aerodynamic resistance.

Tires: High-pressure, very narrow—less than 21 mm wide.

Handlebars: Forearm-supported aerobar allows streamlined aerodynamic position with arms midline and ahead of head.

Brakes: Side- or center-pull.

Saddle: Narrow, often hard.

Pedals: Clipless.

Weight: Under 22 pounds.

MOUNTAIN BIKES

Uses: These bikes are designed for off-road riding: fire roads; single-track (dirt trails with room only for one bike); or wider, double-track (cross-country roads with two best lines). Specialized mountain bikes are used in downhill races.

Mountain bikes are also called all-terrain bikes—ATBs—or off-road bicycles. They offer traction and control on trails, gravel, and sand. Mountain bikes may come with suspension systems: front suspension in the forks or handlebars and rear suspension in the frame design or seat post. Riders sit with an upright posture. These often heavy bikes provide the least aerodynamic efficiency and the most rolling resistance.

Mountain bikes are extremely popular and represent the fastest growing market segment. Though they are designed for off-road use, most riders use them on the road, not on trails.

Frame: Rugged. Smaller than that of a road bike, with a high bottom bracket for increased ground clearance. Larger diameter tubing. Steel, aluminum, titanium, or carbon-fiber tubing.

Gears: Three chain rings. 18–24 gears. Wide range. Index shifting.

Wheels: 26".

Tires: Fat, wide, knobby, low-pressure tires up to 2-¼" wide. Knobbies cope with mud and bumps, but increase friction, making them slower on smooth roads.

Handlebars: Long horizontal bar that is wide and straight, or upswept and angled forward.

Brakes: Cantilever, roller-cam, or U.

Cranks: Longer, for improved leverage.

Pedals: Pedals with sole grips, toeclips and straps, or clipless.

Weight: 20–30 pounds.

TOURING BIKES

Uses: These bikes are designed for multiday touring—trips on which luggage is carried.

Frame: Slightly longer wheelbase than that of a road bicycle, providing more stability with slower handling. Thicker tubing than found on road bicycles. Strong, load bearing. Fixtures for attaching multiple water bottles, fenders, and racks for panniers or saddlebags. Long chainstays help keep the weight of rear panniers in front of the back axle.

Gears: Two or three chain rings. 14–24 gears.

Wheels: 700c. Occasionally, 26".

Tires: 28 mm or 1¼" width common.

Handlebars: Most often dropped, but can be straight.

Brakes: Cantilever, center- or side-pull.

Saddle: Usually padded and wider than found on road bicycles.

Pedals: Toeclips and straps, or clipless.

Weight: Weight 25–32 pounds.

HYBRID BIKES

Uses: Also called cross-terrain, cross, or fitness bikes, they are in between road and mountain bikes. The wheel size and tire frame shape are close to those of a road bike, but the rider's posture is upright because of the mountain bike type of handlebars. Hybrids are often used on the road—especially for commuting and errands—and on smooth, easy trails.

Frame: Lower bottom bracket than found on a mountain bike.

Gears: Two or three chain rings. 14 or more gears.

Wheels: 700c.

Tires: Wider than those of a road-racing bike, but much narrower than the tires of mountain bikes.

Handlebars: Mountain bike style.

Pedals: Toeclips and straps, or clipless.

Weight: 22–26 pounds.

TRACK BIKES

Uses: These bikes are fast-handling but offer low stability. They're used strictly on velodromes (bicycle tracks). They have no brakes. They have a fixed gear—a direct drive with only one gear. To slow and stop a track bike, you apply back pressure on the pedals.

Frame: Lightweight. Narrow wheelbase, steep frame angles.

Gears: One.

Wheels: 700c.

Tires: Narrow, very high pressure.

Handlebars: Drop.

Brakes: None.

Saddle: Narrow, hard.

Cranks: Short for high rpm and clearance of the track banking when the bike is leaned into a turn.

Pedals: Toeclips and single or double straps. Occasionally clipless.

Weight: 15–18 pounds.

RECUMBENTS—HPV BIKES

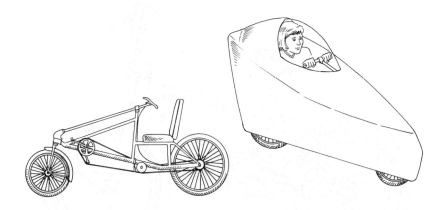

Uses: This unusual bike is low to the ground, and the rider sits reclining, pedaling forward, not down. When used with a wind-cheating cover, or fairing, which makes the bike faster on the level, it's called a human powered vehicle—HPV. The front wheel is usually smaller than the back one. Recumbents offer no aerodynamic benefit; they are slower on climbs, and handling and stability may be worse than that of conventional bikes. Usually ridden on the road, they are less visible to traffic than other types of bikes. In some ways, however, recumbents are more comfortable than upright bicycles. You don't need to crane your neck, and there is less pressure on the crotch. But in other ways they are less comfortable—for example, you can't stand or alternate positions.

Frame: Special design. Steel most common.

Gears: Two chain rings. 14–16 gears.

Wheels: Considerable variation.

EQUIPMENT

Tires: Wider than those of a road-racing bike, but much narrower than the tires of a mountain bike.

Handlebars: Special design.

Seat: Wide, with a back.

Pedals: Toeclips and straps, or clipless.

Weight: 25–35 pounds.

BMX BIKES

Uses: This is a specialized bicycle for bicycle moto-cross courses, generally a sport of children and young adults. The courses offer special jumps and banked turns. BMX bikes are also used for trick riding and for demonstrating bicycle techniques and control—jumps, flips, wheelies, and twists.

Frame: Small, stout, often low-grade heavy steel. High seat post.

Gears: One.

Tires: Medium-width knobby. Small wheels.

Handlebars: High-rise.

Breaks: Coaster.

Pedals: Platform.

Weight: 20–30 pounds.

Uses: A tandem is a bicycle built for two. Tandems come in racing, touring, and mountain bike styles. Bicycles with more than two seats exist but are much less common. The front rider (captain) controls steering, braking, and changing gears. The back rider (stoker) just pedals. Tandems weigh a little less than the combined weight of two bikes, and they offer much less combined wind resistance than two bikes would. They are much faster than a single bike on level ground or downhills, but they have no advantage when it comes to climbing. A tandem provides space for less luggage than two bikes when touring.

Frame: Heavy, long wheelbase. Forks extra thick. Steel, aluminum, or titanium.

Gears: Wide range, two or three chain rings. 14–28 gears.

Wheels: 700c. Occasionally, 26".

Tires: Medium width, high-pressure. Wheels have extra spokes, often as many as 48.

Handlebars: Two pairs, dropped or straight. Handlebars for rear rider (stoker) provide support only.

Brakes: Third brake—drum or disc—often needed for the increased weight, especially for twisty descents or loaded touring.

Saddles: Comfort in the rear is important because of increased jarring and the relative inability to rest the butt off the saddle.

Pedals: Toeclips and straps, or clipless, linked by a timing chain.

Weight: 35–50 pounds.

Uses: Cruisers have a single speed, wide tires, and upright handlebars, sometimes with streamers issuing from the handlebars. This old style of bicycle is most often used for commuting to school or cruising the beach. They're often purchased by collectors or the nostalgic but are gaining popularity among urban commuters.

PEDALS

TYPES OF PEDALS

Everyone knows that when you put pressure on the pedals, the bike goes forward. Most people initially think only about pushing down on the pedals. The simplest platform pedal accomplishes that.

Pedals and the science of pedaling have evolved over the years. The earliest types of pedals—platform pedals—allow you simply to push down.

The next step in pedal evolution was the toeclips and strap system, which allows you also to pull around and up—thus making your pedal stroke more efficient and powerful.

The latest development in pedal technology is the clipless (or toeclip-less) pedal, which allows you to attach your foot firmly (by means of a cleat in your shoe) to the pedal without a constricting toe strap.

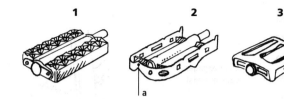

1. *Platform pedal with rubber inserts, for use with ordinary shoes.*
2. *Rat-trap or quill pedal, designed for use with toeclip and strap. The pedal is designed to be used so that the quill faces upward and prevents sideward displacement of the shoe. (a): quill.*
3. *Metal platform pedal.*
4. *Parallel cage pedals, designed to be used either way up. Often found on mountain bikes.*
5. *One type of clipless pedal, designed for a specific cleat system.*

All three kinds of pedals are still available, so let's look at them all in more detail.

Platform Pedals

Either a rubber or quilled metal surface allows friction contact with the shoe to provide some measure of stable contact. These pedals are usually found on BMX and cruiser bikes. They are technically unsophisticated, and no special shoes are needed. They are not very comfortable for long-distance riding.

Platform pedals are good for beginners. No motion is required to engage the shoe, either side of the pedal can be used, the feet can be immediately disengaged from the pedal, and platform pedals are relatively inexpensive.

Toeclips and Straps

Toeclips and straps can be simply and inexpensively added to many platform pedals. They improve the efficiency of pedaling by allowing you to pull up on the pedal stroke. Your foot fits into the toeclip, and when the toe straps are cinched tight, they allow you to pull up on your pedal stroke without your foot coming off the pedal.

Toeclips can be used with or without cleats on your cycling shoes.

Cleats for use with toe-clips are slotted and engage on the rear edge of the pedal. It's best to keep toe straps loose initially, until you're comfortable with the technique for disengaging.

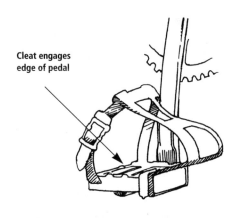

Cleat engages
edge of pedal

Toeclips and straps can be used on almost any type of bicycle. They are still the system of choice for track bicycles, for which two toe straps

Toeclip and strap mounted to metal platform pedal.

are used on each pedal and cinched down tightly to provide extra stability in sprinting.

Toeclip Fit

There should be a millimeter or two—about $\frac{1}{16}$ of an inch—of clearance between the toe of your shoe and the toeclip.

Engaging and Disengaging Toeclips

Getting into toeclips requires a little technique.

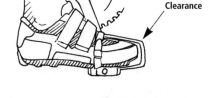

Clearance

Normally, the first foot presents no difficulty. Straddle the bike, engage one shoe while the bike is not moving, and cinch one strap.

The other shoe must be engaged while you are riding: At the bottom of the stroke, using the sole of your shoe, flip the pedal so that the pedal rotates up and allows you to insert your toe into the toeclip. Lean down and cinch your strap.

To get out of toeclips and straps, you must loosen one strap while still in motion. Normally you reach down and release the toe-strap

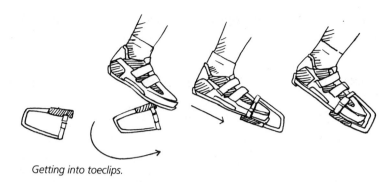

Getting into toeclips.

buckle while your foot is at the top of the pedal stroke. Practice looking ahead, not down at your foot, while doing this.

Riders new to toe clips and straps must make a conscious effort to remember to loosen them before stop signs, traffic lights, and the like, or risk being trapped in their toe clips, losing balance, and falling. After a few rides, this becomes second nature.

Clipless Pedals

These are generally the most expensive type of pedals. They are sometimes called system pedals because they require a compatible shoe and cleat system. Compatible cleats are attached to cycling shoes and snap into or onto the pedals.

Clipless pedals provide more certain contact for most types of riding. They, too, require some technique for getting in and out of them. Once you get used to clipless pedal systems, however, you'll find them more comfortable than the toeclip system, because there

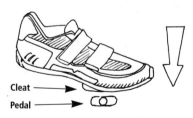

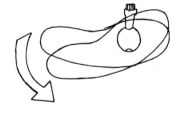

Engaging clipless pedals: Speedplay® system. Simply step down on the pedal.

Disengaging clipless pedals: Twist heel out.

EQUIPMENT

is no strap pressing on the tops of your feet. "Floating" clipless pedals allow the foot to rotate while engaged. This helps prevent some types of knee problems. Using floating pedals initially feels like "walking on ice" and requires some practice before they can be used confidently.

Some clipless system pedals are engaged by first inserting the forward part of the cleat into the pedal. Others engage by first inserting the rear of the cleat. For still others, no toe-in or heel-in technique is required. Disengagement is usually accomplished most easily at the bottom of the pedal stroke by turning the heel outward. Some systems disengage more easily at other points in the pedal stroke; some disengage more easily by turning the heel inward. You'll have to read the instructions that come with your system, ask others, or experiment with your system to see which method works best.

Just as with toeclips, when you are learning to ride with a clipless system, be extra careful approaching stop signs and traffic lights, and be ready to disengage one foot. Falling over in slow motion is certainly entertaining for passersby, but it can be avoided with a little practice. The benefits of a clipless pedal system are many: Your foot won't accidentally slip off the pedal if you hit a bump in the road. With proper cleat placement, your foot will be perfectly positioned to transfer maximum power to the pedals. You will be able to push down and pull up efficiently. You won't have to worry about releasing toe straps before disengaging your shoe. And, perhaps least important, you'll look like a serious cyclist!

RIDING ACCESSORIES

Sure, the bike's the main thing. But there are many accessories for your bicycle. Bicycle accessories make riding safer, more comfortable, and more fun. Starred items* are considered essential.

HELMETS*

Helmets are not only an essential accessory but are required by law in some states, and they are required for participation in most organized bicycle rides. They are inexpensive, and one of the best small investments you'll ever make. Get one and wear it every time you ride. Before

I agree to coach riders, they agree to wear a helmet at all times when on their bicycles.

- Helmets protect your head in the event of a crash. There is no question that helmets save lives and reduce injury. Almost all bicycle helmets sold today meet Snell or ANSI testing standards.
- They have reflective materials for improving nighttime visibility.
- They improve aerodynamics and speed.
- Studies have shown that well-ventilated helmets do not cause overheating.

SHORTS

Although not all real men eat quiche, they do parade around in those slinky black Lycra shorts. When I taught my wife how to ride she was eager for any adventure. "But," she asked, "do I have to wear those black things?" Now she wouldn't think of riding without them.

There's good reason to get a good pair of bicycling shorts. Wearing underwear underneath them, however, defeats some of their advantages.

- Bicycling shorts don't have seams where you sit on them, so they don't irritate your rear end.
- They breathe.
- They fit snugly, which means that, unlike regular shorts, there is no free edge to rub and chafe your inner thighs.
- Traditional shorts are black. A bike rider occasionally needs to wipe dirty hands on something—say, after fixing a flat tire—and black shorts fit the bill. Additionally, some black leather seats make shorts darker. Black ones don't show the discoloration.
- Bicycling shorts are padded in the right places to help prevent saddle sores.
- The tightness of the Lycra allows small objects to be held under the fabric against a leg.

JERSEYS

- Bright colors improve visibility.
- Back pockets carry small articles securely and safely.

EQUIPMENT

21

- Aerodynamics and speed are improved by their tight, nonbillowing fit.
- Moisture is wicked away by modern materials to keep you cooler on hot days, warmer on cool days.

SHOES

Bicycling shoes increase your cycling enjoyment. There are different types of bicycling shoes for dedicated road riding, touring, and mountain biking. All bicycling shoes have the advantages listed below. The nonrecessed cleats on road bike shoes make walking uncomfortable and a little dangerous. Mountain biking and touring shoes, sometimes slightly heavier than road bike shoes, have a recessed cleat that allows relatively comfortable, safe walking.

- Bicycling shoes have cleats to engage the pedal.
- They improve your efficiency by allowing you to pull upward on the pedal.
- They improve comfort.
- Their stiff soles and stable base improve the transmission force to the pedal.

SOCKS

Although not everyone wears them, bike-specific or athletic socks increase comfort, reduce chafing and blisters, and help absorb and wick up moisture.

GLOVES

- Gloves improve hand comfort and help prevent nerve damage from the jarring of the handlebars.
- They help prevent cuts and abrasions in the event of a fall.
- They often have a terry cloth backing for wiping sweat or a runny nose.
- They improve the grip on the handlebars.

EYEWEAR

Sunglasses not only reduce glare and improve eye comfort but also protect the eye from dust and other airborne debris. On cloudy days, clear lenses are important for eye safety and comfort.

WEATHER GEAR

Wet- and cold-weather gear makes cycling more enjoyable when it's not sunny and warm out. A windbreaker or cycling vest helps keep out the wind chill. Long-sleeved jerseys and tights often provide the initial defense against cold weather. Use long-fingered gloves for your hands on cold days and cycling shoe covers or booties for the feet. A headband or helmet liner helps keep your ears toasty.

Polypropylene and other advanced fibers wick the wet from your skin and help keep you warm and dry. Waterproof rain jackets, leggings, gloves, and waterproof helmet liners and booties are often lifesavers on wet-weather touring trips.

PUMP*

Lightweight bicycle pumps attach to the frame and allow you to fix flat tires or pump up slow leaks. They require periodic maintenance to ensure that their gaskets do not dry out.

SMALL SADDLEBAG

A small saddlebag, fitting under the saddle, provides space for a tube, a few tools, repair kit, cash, ID, sunscreen, and lip balm.

TUBE REPAIR KIT*

A small tire repair kit with tire irons allows you to fix flats. The tire irons are helpful for removing the tire from the wheel. Modern kits have patches that stick without having to apply messy glue. It's also a good idea to carry an extra bicycle tube or two, so you can replace the tube if you get a flat and fix the puncture at home.

TOOLS*

- Allen keys: The 5-mm one is commonly needed for adjusting seat height. If this is not your bike's seatpost bolt size, get what you need. Other common sizes used on bicycles are 2 mm, 4 mm, and 6 mm.

- A small crescent wrench, screwdrivers, spoke wrench, and chain tool may be useful.
- A bicycle combination tool usually includes 4-mm, 5-mm, and 6-mm Allen keys, and flat-head and Phillips screwdrivers.
- Bicycle touring requires a more extensive kit.

CASH

Stopping midway on your ride for a snack? Need an emergency part from a bike store en route? Or a taxi to rescue you? They may take a credit card, but cash is always accepted.

EMERGENCY ID*

Carry emergency ID—your name and address, a copy of your health insurance card, and emergency contact number, medical information alerts if you have allergies or significant medical conditions. Keep these copies in your small saddlebag so that they'll always be available.

Hide your name and address somewhere on your bike, perhaps in your seat tube. Include a notice such as this one: "This bike may be stolen. Please contact . . ." Include your name, address, and telephone number. This may help identify your bike if it is stolen or alert a bike mechanic.

WATER BOTTLES AND CAGES

Riding for more than half an hour? Attach a water bottle cage to your frame and get a water bottle. If planning on rides longer than an hour, especially in the heat, get two.

BIKE COMPUTER AND HEART-RATE MONITOR

Computers are available that can give speed, average speed, distance traveled, elapsed time, cadence, current altitude, elevation gained or lost, temperature, and heart rate. Current speed and distance traveled are the most important features; they're incorporated into almost all bicycle computers. Even beginning riders get a kick out of seeing how fast they're going or how far they've gone.

Separate heart-rate monitors are also available. Many enthusiasts like being able to monitor this measure of cycling intensity.

MIRROR

Mirrors that attach to the helmet or handlebar help riders have "eyes in the back of their heads" to monitor traffic or other riders. With a slight movement of the head, helmet-mounted mirrors allow a cyclist to see more of the road behind. Those that attach to the handlebar may have blind spots.

LIGHTS

Seeing and being seen are important. A flashing rear light is a good safety item. You may not plan on riding at dusk, or in the dark, but it's easy to be surprised by nightfall. Flashing rear lights provide good visibility, weigh almost nothing, and use very little battery power.

Front lights, which help you see and be seen by others, require a lot of wattage to truly light up the road. Although regular batteries can power a front light for occasional use on suburban streets, serious, safe nighttime commuting, touring, racing, or mountain biking requires a beefy system. You may get by with 5 watts, but 10 watts or more really do make a difference. When my wife got a powerful 30-watt halogen system, she really started enjoying riding at night. And cars gave her a lot more respect—they thought she was riding a motorcycle.

BIKE LOCKS

The best deterrent to theft is not to leave your bicycle out of your sight. Get a window seat at the coffee shop, hide your bike in a closet at work, or bring it into the grocery store.

But if you must park your bike out of your immediate sight, a bike lock may help prevent theft. Two locks, of different types, may provide more of a deterrent. Most locks can be destroyed by a determined thief.

HOW BICYCLES WORK

THE GREATEST INVENTION SINCE THE WHEEL

Of course, the bicycle is actually two wheels, mounted to a frame. It is the most efficient means of transportation in existence. Here, the essential workings of a "standard" bike are described—specialty bicycles may operate differently.

EQUIPMENT

THE BASIC ANATOMY OF A BICYCLE

The bicycle frame (A) is the skeleton that supports the rest of the bicycle and the rider. The fork (B) supports the front wheel. The seat

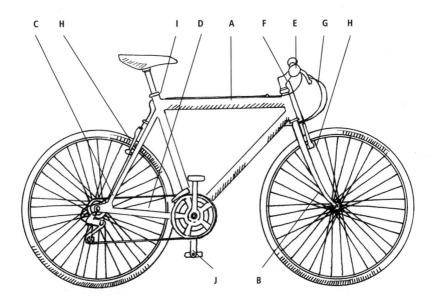

A typical bicycle.

stays (C) and chain stays (D) support the rear wheel. Handlebars (E) are attached to the frame with a stem (F). The seat is attached to the frame via the seat post (I).

The pedals are attached to the cranks (J). Brake levers (G) are attached to the handlebars and have cables to the brakes (H), which are attached to the frame.

PARTS OF A FRAME

Frames are commonly made of steel, aluminum, titanium, or carbon fiber.

The main tubes of a frame are the top tube (A), down tube (B), and seat tube (C).

The head tube (D) is a short tube connecting the top tube and down tube. It contains the steering tube (E), an extension of the front fork (F). The front wheel is attached to the fork at the front dropouts (G).

The bottom bracket (H) joins the down tube and seat tube, and the

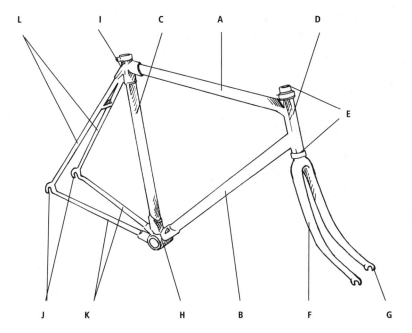

The bicycle frame.

seat post (I) enters the frame at the junction of the top tube and down tube. The rear wheel is attached at the rear dropouts (J), formed by the stays. The stays from the bottom bracket are the chain stays (K); the stays from the seat post are the seat stays (L). The stays form the rear triangle, together with the seat tube.

MOVING FORWARD

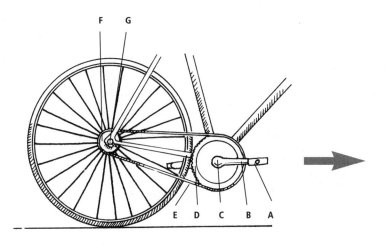

How your muscles make the bicycle move forward.

You use the muscles of your legs to push the pedals (a). The pedals are connected to crank arms (b) that rotate on an axle (c). A toothed gear (the chain ring, d) drives the chain (e). The rear wheel has an attached cog or sprocket gear (rear-wheel cog, f). The moving chain drives the cog and forces the wheel to rotate on its axle (g).

HOW GEARS WORK

Gears allow each crank or chain ring revolution to result in a different number of rear-wheel revolutions. That is, turning the crank (and thus turning the chain ring) results in a different number of turns of the rear-wheel cog for each gear setting.

If the number of teeth on the chain ring (in front) and the number of teeth on the rear-wheel cog (in back) are the same, then one revolution of the chain ring will result in one revolution of the rear wheel. This is the situation when you use a small chain ring with 24 teeth and a rear cog with the same number of teeth.

Suppose the number of the teeth on the chain ring is four times the number of teeth on the cog. Now turning the chain ring makes the rear wheel turn around four times. That makes it much harder to pedal than when the number of teeth are the same. The four-times factor occurs with a chain ring with 52 teeth and a 13-tooth cog.

A one-to-one ratio might be suitable for climbing hills with touring packs or on a mountain bike; the four-to-one ratio is typical for very fast racers on flat terrain, or riders riding with a tailwind or going downhill.

The range from one-to-one to about four-to-one is typical for bicycle touring. The majority of riders, most of the time, will use a range of gears between those two extremes.

Most road bicycles have two chain rings and seven or eight cogs. Most touring and mountain bikes have three chain rings—the third, a very small chain ring, makes it easier to get up hills when you're loaded down with panniers or climbing steep slopes. If you live in a hilly area, it's reasonable to have a third ring even on a road bike—it just makes life easier.

Gear-Inches Defined

Bicycles have different size wheels. Most road bicycles have wheels with a nominal diameter of 700 millimeters (referred to as 700c), about

27 inches. By nominal I mean that they're not really exactly that size. Most mountain bikes have wheels with a nominal diameter of 26 inches. Since 4 revolutions of a larger wheel will mean the bicycle travels farther than 4 revolutions of a smaller wheel, the effect of wheel size is considered when discussing the difficulty of a gear. If you multiply the ratio of the chain ring to the cog by the size of the wheel, you get a more accurate picture of the degree of difficulty of a particular gear.

For a 27-inch wheel, if the chain ring and cog have the same number of teeth, the gear selected is 27 gear-inches. If the chain ring has 52 teeth and the cog 13, for a four-to-one ratio, the number of gear-inches is 4 x 27 = 108.

On a mountain bike with 26-inch wheels, if the chain ring has 52 teeth and the cog 13, for a four-to-one ratio, the number of gear-inches is 4 x 26 = 104.

Gear-Inches in Typical Setups

Most road bicycles have two chain rings and seven or eight cogs on the rear wheel. The small chain ring typically has 39 or 42 teeth. The

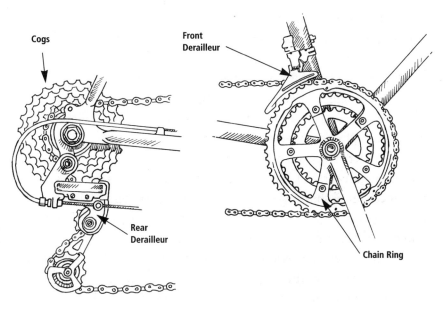

Cogs

Front Derailleur

Rear Derailleur

Chain Ring

Rear gears, rear derailleur

Front gears, front derailleur

large chain ring typically has 53 teeth. The cogs typically range from 12 to 28 teeth, although racers frequently use 12 to 21 teeth.

This means that the easiest gear to pedal in a typical setup is "39-28," for about 38 gear-inches. The hardest gear is typically "53-12," for about 119 gear-inches.

Mountain bicycles have three chain rings and seven or eight cogs on the rear wheel. The smallest chain ring typically has 20 to 24 teeth. The large chain ring typically has 40 to 46 teeth. The cogs typically range from 12 to 24 teeth.

On a mountain bike the easiest gear to pedal might be "24-24," for 26 gear-inches. The hardest, "46-12," would be 95 gear-inches.

Basic Gear Rule

Some cyclists find it interesting to figure things out exactly. In fact, some riders seem to spend more hours figuring out the exact gear-inches of all their gears than they do riding. But it's not necessary to know the exact gear-inches of each one of your gears. There is a basic rule for beginners: More teeth on the chain ring in the front—harder to pedal. More teeth on the cogs in the back—easier to pedal.

For climbing a hill, you normally use the small chain ring in front and a big cog in back. For downhills and tailwinds it's just the opposite—a big chain ring in the front and a small cog in the back.

Derailleurs—How Gears are Shifted

The workings of derailleurs—the gear-shifting mechanisms—can be easily understood. Although the exact mechanisms of derailleurs may differ, they all operate on the same principle. A derailleur moves the chain to different gears. The derailleur is pulled either in or out by cables that originate near the front of the bicycle, where the rider operates them with mechanical shifting levers. Some derailleur shifters are located on the down tube, some twist on the handlebar, and some are incorporated into the brake levers.

When the cable is released, the derailleurs move through spring action. The design of the derailleur incorporates limit screws to restrict the travel or movement of the derailleur. This prevents the derailleur from moving, or shifting, the chain too far over the gears, into the bicycle frame, pedals, or wheel.

TIRES

As those in the Stone Age found, the round wheel is great for reducing rolling resistance. Tires, or outside casings, contain a tube that holds air. Riding on a cushion of air rather than a solid tire dramatically improves rolling resistance and comfort.

There is a "right" amount of tire pressure for any given tire and any given use. Too little air pressure in the tire makes it feel squishy, allows it to roll too easily on its rim, and reduces stability. Too much air pressure produces a harsh ride and decreases the contact patch—or area on the tire that comes in contact with the ground—reducing stability.

The choice of tires is a compromise of different needs:

- Stability is improved with wider tires and "moderate" tire pressures.

- Aerodynamic resistance is improved with narrower tires.

- Durability and puncture resistance are improved with quality materials, tighter weaves, extra plies and belts, and "moderate" tire pressures.

- Rolling resistance is improved with quality materials, tighter weaves, fewer plies and belts, and high tire pressures.

- Cost is increased with quality materials, tighter weaves, extra plies, and belts.

STEERING

Turning the front wheel steers the bicycle. The handlebars are attached to the stem. The stem in turn is attached to the steerer tube, which runs down through the head tube to the fork, which holds the front wheel in place. There is a direct mechanical connection between turning the handlebar and turning the front wheel.

Although steering is important in turning a bicycle, it is not the only factor. The shifting of body weight and the angle at which you lean the bicycle also affect turning.

BRAKES

By squeezing the brake levers mounted on the handlebar, you pull on the brake cables. The cables run in cable housings to the brakes. The brake for the front wheel is located on the front fork; the brake for the rear wheel is located on the seat stays.

When a cable is shortened, it pulls the two sides of the brake closer together, squeezing the brake pads against the rim. The friction of the brake pads on the rim slows the turning of the wheel and the bicycle. When the brake levers are released, the cable lengthens. Spring action releases the brake pads.

BRAKE CABLE ADJUSTMENT

Cable length is initially set, with tools, at the brake fixing bolt. You can also make fine and coarse adjustments to the brake cable without tools on most brakes. These adjustments are made by turning an adjusting barrel with your fingers or flicking a simple cam mechanism.

You'll want to adjust your brakes to:

- Compensate for the stretching of the brake cable, which occurs over time.
- Allow the substitution of a different wheel with a different rim width.
- Allow fat tires to pass through the brake pads when removing the wheel.

BICYCLE FIT

The right size bicycle is important. It allows you to be comfortable, ride safely, and work effectively. It makes you a better rider.

If a bicycle is too big or too small for you, you may lose control and fall. When you stand over the bicycle, there should always be some clearance between the top tube and your crotch. If your crotch touches the top tube, the bicycle is certainly too big.

FRAME SIZE

Frames are sized on the length of the seat tube. The size frame you need is most closely related to the length of your leg. The precise way in which manufacturers size their frames, however, varies.

Top Tube Length

Although frame size is the most important factor in choosing the frame that is right for you, different manufacturers also have different length top tubes for the same size frame.

Women have shorter upper bodies and need relatively shorter top tubes than men. Some adjustment can be made to the effective length of the top tube by the use of handlebar stems of different length.

Frame size: Allow at least 1 inch of clearance between the top tube and your crotch for a road bike.

Choosing Your Frame Size

A number of methods exist for determining frame size: To determine your inseam measurement, stand with your back to a wall with the spine of a 1-inch-thick book against your inner leg, snug against your crotch. Measure from the floor to the top edge of the book. Most racing bicycles are sold in metric sizes. One inch is 2.54 centimeters. If you used inches, convert to metric by multiplying by 2.54. For a road bicycle, authorities advocate a frame size that is 65 to 67 percent of your inseam. For example, my inseam is 30 inches, or 76 centimeters. Based on the formula, I should ride a 50-cm bike.

When you stand over a road bicycle, there should be 1 inch of clearance from the top tube to your crotch in stocking feet, and about 1 to 2 inches when you're wearing shoes.

If you are sizing a mountain bike, you'll need another inch of clearance over the top tube.

POSITION ON THE BICYCLE

Although there are general principles, the final decision regarding position must be made by the individual.

Position is a compromise. Position is different for optimizing muscle power, aerobic efficiency, comfort, and bicycle control and for minimizing injury.

Here are some simple ways to make sure your position is not "too far off."

Be Safe

Never make adjustments to bicycle parts that extend them beyond their safe limits. The stem and seatpost normally have limit lines marked with either "maximum extension" or "minimum insertion" warnings.

Be certain to tighten bolts properly after making adjustments.

Where to Start

The order in which you perform adjustments is important, since some measurements are dependent upon others. This order works best for most riders:

Foot-Pedal Fore-Aft: If you use cleats, the cleat should be positioned so that the ball of the foot is over the pedal spindle.

Seat Height: Many road riders place the heel of their shoe on the pedal and set the seat height so that the heel just touches the pedal. I've found that a knee angle of 25 to 30 degrees from full extension when the leg is at the bottom of the stroke is a good compromise between performance and injury prevention.

Since bicycle control is a little better with the seat slightly lower, mountain bikers may adjust their seat height down to allow up to 5 degrees more bend in the knee.

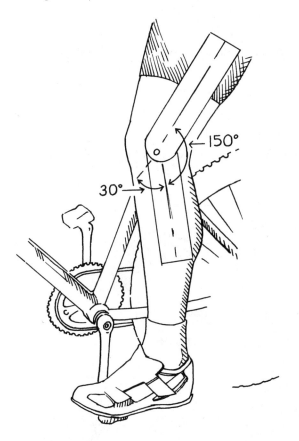

Seat height: A seat height that results in a knee angle of 25 to 30 degrees from full extension is a good compromise.

Seat Position Fore-Aft: When the cranks are horizontal, a plumb line from the front of the knees should fall through the pedal axle.

Seat Angle: Most riders ride best when their seat is level. Some have the noses of their saddles up or slightly down. Slightly down often helps with crotch discomfort in women or with the use of aerobars—but too far down will result in more pressure on your arms and hands.

Foot/Pedal Rotation Angle: The cleat should be positioned so that your

EQUIPMENT

toes point nearly straight ahead. Some riders prefer their feet pointed slightly in, some slightly out. You may wish to ride a little with your cleats slightly loose, and see where you are most comfortable before final tightening. Cleat position is not as critical with free-rotation systems, which allow your foot to rotate while still fixing it fore-aft, side-to-side, and up-and-down.

In general, if the outside of your knee hurts, adjust your cleats to point your toes a little more outward. If the inside of your knee hurts, point your toes a little more inward.

Handlebar Width: Handlebar width for road bicycles should be roughly the width of your shoulders.

Handlebar Angle: The handlebars of road bicycles should be angled so that they are perpendicular to your seat tube. This means that they are pointed down about 15 degrees.

Brake Levers: Road bicycle brake levers are most comfortable when

Stem extension: Two rules of thumb: With the hands in the drops, (1) the stem should result in just a little clearance between your elbow and knee, and (2) the top of the handlebar should just hide the front hub.

positioned such that their tips are in line with the bottom of the handlebar drops.

Stem Height: The stem is usually best 1 to 3 inches below the height of your saddle. It's set at the higher level for mountain biking and climbing on road bikes, at the lower level for flat or rolling road riding.

Stem Extension: Most bikes are sized so that the majority of men end up needing stems 10 to 13 cm in length and most women end up needing stems several centimeters shorter. On a road bicycle, when your hands are in the drops of the handlebars there should be scant clearance between your elbows and your knees.

A rule of thumb is that with the hands in the drops, the top of the handlebars obscures the front axle when you're looking down.

SAFETY

Bicycle accidents and injuries are a source of concern for all of us. The truth is that most accidents are preventable. Most people, when asked what the number one safety issue is for bicyclists, say that they are most concerned about dangerous, unpredictable cars. Perhaps that is because an unpredictable motorist is an area of vulnerability over which most cyclists have little control. Perhaps it is because accidents involving bicycles and cars have the potential to be the most serious. But bicycle-car collisions, though they are usually the most serious, account for only 10 to 20 percent of accidents. Falls account for about 50 percent of accidents, bicycle-bicycle collisions 10 to 20 percent, and bike-dog encounters and other causes make up the remainder.

Four main topics govern safety. Most of these can be easily attended to and most risks minimized:

1. Keep bicycle equipment safe—well maintained and in mechanically sound working order.

2. Acquire the riding skills and techniques to operate a bicycle safely.

3. Know how bicycle-car accidents commonly occur. Ride in a safe and defensive manner.

4. Use specialized safety equipment.

MAKING YOUR BICYCLE EQUIPMENT SAFE

Just as you take your car for tune-ups and oil changes, have a bicycle mechanic check out your bike at least every six months for safety and performance. Proper fit, installation, reliability, and maintenance of equipment are essential for rider safety and performance. Equipment must be clean, adjusted, and lubricated. Lightweight or aerodynamic equipment should not be used if safety is sacrificed. All riders should familiarize themselves with basic maintenance. No matter who works on your bike, you must check it and be confident of its safety.

The basic principles of bicycle equipment safety are that the wheels and other parts should be tightly fastened to the frame, the wheels should be sound, the tires should be properly inflated, the brakes and gears should work, and the drive train should move freely.

MAINTENANCE CHECKLIST

Frame: The frame must be straight or aligned. It must have no cracks.

Wheels: The wheels should be true. (In other words, they should not wobble when you spin them.) When fastened to the frame, the wheels should turn freely, without play. You should have no loose spokes. If bolts fasten the wheels to the frame, they must be tight. Quick-release skewers (which are levered closed, not screwed) can be adjusted with a nut on the end opposite the lever if they are loose. When you are closing the quick-release lever, you should start feeling some resistance when it is at a 45-degree angle to the frame. Inadequate tightening of a quick-release skewer is a common cause of a wheel coming loose from the frame.

Tires: Tires should be properly inflated. Replace the tire if casing or sidewall cuts are present. Check for hidden glass in the tread. There should be no bulges or tire cords showing. Tires get old and cracked with time, even when not ridden.

Headset: Must be adjusted so that it is free to move without play. It must not be pitted or it will stick in certain positions, most commonly straight ahead.

Bottom Bracket: Should be adjusted to move freely without play.

Crank Set: Crank bolts must be tight.

Brakes: The brake levers must be secure and immovable with moderate side pressure. The levers should not depress as far as the handlebar and they should return freely when released. The brake pads must be adjusted correctly, simultaneously hitting the rim surfaces, not the tires. The brake pads need replacing when worn beyond their wear lines.

Cables: The cables should not be frayed or torn, and their housing not kinked. Broken cable strands mean that the whole cable must be replaced.

Seat Post: The post must be aligned and the seatpost bolt must be tight.

Saddle: The seat must be aligned straight ahead, the seat bolts tight.

Drive Train: All gears must be working. The chain must not derail from either the chain rings or the rear sprockets. Test on uphill grades or with pressure to ensure cog/chain compatibility. Derailleurs must be fastened securely to the frame and be adjusted so as not to shift the chain into the spokes or into the chain stay. There should be no stiff links in the chain.

Handlebars: These should be securely fastened. Full body weight on the hoods, or aerobars if used, should not result in any slippage. Handlebar plugs should be present at the bar ends.

Stem: Fastened securely.

Pedals: These must be fastened securely to the cranks. They should rotate freely. "Clipless pedals" need slight lubrication at the pedal-engagement springs. Check that the shoe engages and disengages as desired. Adjust pedal tension if needed.

Water Bottle Cages: Securely fastened. No cracks in welds or bends.

Accessories (such as pannier racks, lights, and fenders): Securely fastened. No cracks in welds or bends.

Shoes: Cleats securely fastened and not overly worn. Velcro, laces, or other closures strong, functioning well, and not dangling.

After any adjustments or work is done on your bicycle, it's always a good idea to test it out with a spin around the block. Try all your gears,

SAFETY

stand up on a little hill—make sure everything is in good working order. Do not wait until the day of your "big" ride to try it out.

RIDING SKILLS

RIDING IN A STRAIGHT LINE

This is an important and basic skill. Although many racers think they can perform this skill easily, most are surprised at the level of skill required to ride the black (inside) line of a velodrome at 30 miles per hour.

Riding "Aerobars"

Riding aerobars—forearm-supported bars—especially with crosswinds, requires special skills, including relearning how to ride in a straight line:

- Relax the body, especially your arms, bending them at the elbow. Freezing up and overreacting causes most problems.
- Look ahead at where you want to go, not right down at the road, at potholes, or other places you wish to avoid.
- Control is a matter of learning how the bike responds when you lean your body, lean the bike, or steer.
- Steer forearm-supported bars with the body, not with the hands.
- Practice turning in an area without traffic. Ride in S-curves, purposefully weaving back and forth around a real or imagined line. This helps you learn the effects of shifts in body weight on steering.

LOOKING BACK WHILE RIDING

Looking back is important when riding in traffic to check on cars and when racing to check on other racers. Beginning riders may have difficulty riding in a straight line, maintaining pace, and looking back all at the same time.

Looking over the Shoulder

Beginners tend to veer to the left when they look over their left shoulder, because the tendency is to redistribute weight to the turned side or turn the upper body and consequently the handlebars.

- When looking over the left shoulder, relax the handlebar grip with the left arm or drop the left shoulder.

- Sliding your rear end slightly to the right side helps keep the weight centered over the bicycle.
- Riding with a partner one or two bike lengths behind and slightly to the left of you gives a focus target.
- The following rider can give feedback about maintaining a straight line and speed.
- At first, just glance back.
- Build up to looking back for several seconds.
- Repeat looking back over the right shoulder.
- Maintain speed.
- Practice looking back using a hand placed on a rider beside you. This helps you maintain a straight line.

Looking under the Arm

Looking back under the shoulder when riding allows a rider to maintain an aerodynamic position riding in the drops. Practice looking under a shoulder alone or with a partner behind you to provide a focus target.

SIGNALING TO MOTORISTS

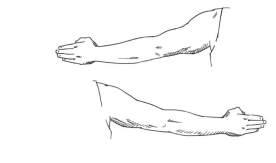

Hand signals: Signal turns with the appropriate outstretched hand. A stop is signaled with the left arm pointing down.

Signal a left turn with an outstretched left arm. Signal a right turn with an outstretched right arm. A stop can be signaled with a downward left arm, palm backward, although it is often safer to have both hands on the handlebar when stopping.

Don't be shy about shouting loudly, and, of course, politely to motorists. For example, if you think a motorist is about to pull out in front of you and hasn't seen you, a loud *"Watch out!"* can be heard even with car windows closed.

BRAKING

The front brake has more stopping power than the rear. The rear contributes to slowing the bike and prevents flipping over the handlebars, and should also be used.

Position helps maintain control, especially in emergency situations such as when a car pulls out in front of you. Slide back in the saddle to weight the rear wheel. The cranks should be horizontal, or your lead foot slightly up. On a road bike, your hands should be in the drops and the arms braced.

Both brakes should be applied at the same time. In emergency braking, you should brake harder with the front brake while you continue to brake as usual with the rear. Learn the consequences of overbraking with either brake. When the rear wheel skids, for example, it can be because it is locked up and you need to let up on the rear brake. But normally the rear wheel skids because there is too much weight being transferred forward—the rear wheel is being unweighted—and you need to let up on the front brake.

Practice braking under safe and controlled circumstances and you'll feel more confident braking in emergencies.

DOGS

When chased or attacked by a dog while riding:

- Do not take your feet out of the pedals. This gives dogs an attractive target.
- Not pedaling may lessen the legs as a target. Alternatively, sprinting may remove you as a target!

- Riding in a straight line usually works best. This is especially important when traffic is present.
- Barking and biting dogs are territorial. They will usually leave you alone as soon as you are past their owner's property line.
- Many of the most vicious dogs are trained. A firm, sharp command like *"Sit!"* may get them to do just that.
- Some riders squirt liquid from their water bottles or threaten dogs with their frame pumps. For most of us, it is probably best to keep control of the bike with both hands on the bars and get out of their "territory" as quickly as possible.

OBSTACLES

Avoiding obstacles by riding safely around them is always the preferred course of action. Small obstacles such as small potholes, branches, or cattle grates can be ridden over. With your cranks horizontal, hands in the drops if you have them, unweight your rear end off the saddle. Much less force will be transmitted to damage the bicycle or jar you.

Try to avoid ridges and slots that are aligned with your direction of travel. If you can't avoid them, try to ride perpendicularly across them, as traffic allows.

Crossing Railroad Tracks

Tracks perpendicular to the roadway can often be safely crossed. Try to cross diagonal tracks by riding perpendicularly across them, if traffic allows.

Some tracks are too dangerous to be crossed without dismounting and walking across them.

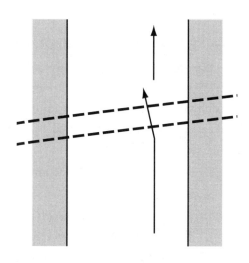

Crossing railroad tracks: Ride perpendicularly to diagonal tracks.

Jumping Obstacles

This is an advanced riding skill that may be necessary if it is not possible to go around a dangerous obstacle.

The easiest position in which to jump an obstacle is with your cranks horizontal, hands in the drops if you have them, the rear end unweighted off the saddle.

Lower your profile by crouching down, then jump up, pulling the bike up to you.

You can raise the front wheel without cleats or toeclips. But they are necessary for raising the rear wheel.

In order to learn this skill:

- Practice at first off the bicycle, pretending to be in a riding position, feet horizontal. Crouch down and jump up.

- On the bike, practice raising the front wheel by pulling up on the handlebars.

- To practice raising the rear wheel, have your rear end off the saddle while crouched, jump up, pull up with the feet.

- Practice raising both wheels together.

- Pick lines in the road and practice jumping them, then practice jumping small objects like broomsticks. Move up to small rocks and curbs, practicing until you are comfortable.

HOW BICYCLE-CAR ACCIDENTS OCCUR

Here are some of the common reasons cars hit bicycles, or vice versa. By examining these common situations, you can learn defensive lessons. Riding safely can prevent most injuries.

1. A bicyclist enters a road from a driveway, lane, or other road without looking.

2. A bicyclist turns left into an intersection without first checking for vehicles.

3. A bicyclist riding on the sidewalk exits at a driveway without first checking for a following vehicle.

4. A bicyclist rides on a narrow road without a shoulder. The bicyclist is to the extreme right of the road. A passing vehicle may

either hit the bicyclist or push the bicyclist off the road into a curb or ditch.

5. A bicyclist swerves into a lane of traffic to avoid an obstruction without checking for vehicles.

6. Riding at night without sufficient illumination, a bicyclist may be hit by a vehicle entering the road from a driveway, lane, or other road.

7. A bicyclist riding close to a parked car may run into an opening car door.

8. A bicyclist may run into the back of a vehicle that stops suddenly.

9. A bicyclist stops at an intersection where the left lane of traffic may proceed left or straight. The bicyclist is on the right side of this lane. The bicyclist turns left. A vehicle accelerating straight through the intersection may hit the bicyclist.

10. A bicyclist stops at an intersection where the left lane of traffic may proceed left or straight. The bicyclist is on the left side of this lane. The bicyclist turns left. A vehicle also turns left. The bicyclist is trapped, unable to move to the right side of the road, and may be hit.

11. A vehicle, pedestrian, or animal, hidden by a parked vehicle, moves out into the road and into a bicyclist's path.

12. A bicyclist rides up to a red light on the inside of a line of stopped vehicles. The first vehicle in line is a bus or truck. The bicyclist is in the driver's blind spot. The driver may turn right into the bicyclist.

13. A bicyclist may be hit at night by a following vehicle.

14. An oncoming vehicle may turn right into a bicyclist after a break in traffic. The oncoming traffic has hidden the bicyclist from the view of the turning vehicle.

15. A vehicle passes a bicyclist to make a turn. The bicyclist is moving faster than the vehicle anticipates, and the vehicle may turn into the cyclist.

16. At a crossroads, a driver sees a break in traffic but does not see the bicyclist. The vehicle may run into the bicyclist.

A SAFE AND DEFENSIVE RIDING STYLE

Here are a few rules of defensive riding that can help you prepare for and avoid the situations listed above.

- Know and obey the traffic rules. The bicycle is treated as a vehicle in most states. Learn the local bicycle laws and regulations.

- You are sharing the road with others. Respect the rights of others and be tolerant if they trespass on yours.

- Assume that motorists will not see you. They expect and look for other motorists and often have a "blind eye" for cyclists. Always assume that a motorist will do something imprudent—for example, pull out in front of you.

- Look ahead of your current position. Don't just look at the roadway beneath you. Anticipate possible problems down the road.

- Ride only one person on a bicycle unless you're on a tandem or other special bicycle.

- Ride on the right side of the road, so that you're riding with traffic, not on the left, where you'd be riding against traffic. Never ride on the sidewalk.

- Do not ride against traffic on one-way streets.

- A busy, narrow stretch of road where you need complete control of the bicycle is not a good place to take out your water bottle for a drink. Keep both hands on the handlebars. Do not ride no-hands.

- Use lights when riding at night.

- Do not ride through stop signs or red lights.

- Don't hitch rides by holding on to other vehicles.

- Never ride under the influence of drugs or alcohol.

- Signal turns.

- Ride predictably, in a straight line at a steady pace.

- Yield to larger roads.

- Look left, right, and left again before entering roads or intersections.

- Make eye contact with drivers.

- When riding alongside parked cars, look through rear windows to see drivers and anticipate opening car doors.

- Even though you have the right of way, do not insist upon it. Cars have much better protection against accidents than you do; you are more likely to be hurt than the motorist.

Remember, just because you make eye contact with a motorist, it does not mean that the motorist "sees" you. In some circumstances, it is not safe to cross an intersection even with the right-of-way green light. If you cannot make eye contact and the motorist is edging forward, looking the other way, proceed very slowly, if at all, across the intersection. Shouting a friendly warning may get the driver's attention.

Traffic-light sensors do not always respond to bicycles. The light may not change unless a vehicle behind approaches close enough to the intersection to trip the sensor, or you press a pedestrian cross button.

RIDING ALONG THE ROAD

Here are some practical tips for safer street riding:
- The width of the road determines the safest place to ride. In general, ride at least 1 foot from the curb. This helps prevent being squeezed against the curb or into a ditch, avoids significant road debris, and gives you room to maneuver in case of a gust of wind from the side. Riding a bit away from the curb also allows motorists to see you better.

- When parked cars are present, if the width of the overall road permits, ride 3 to 4 feet away from them to avoid opening doors, cars, pedestrians, and others entering the road.

- When riding next to a row of parked cars, ride in a straight line; avoid weaving into spaces between cars. To do so makes you less visible to traffic.

Parked cars: Ride a straight line to the edge of parked cars. Leave enough room for opening car doors if the width of the roadway is adequate. When parked cars form an interrupted line, avoid darting in and out—to do so reduces your visibility to motorists and increases the danger.

- Perhaps counterintuitively, when the width of the road narrows, it may be safer to ride more out in the lane to force vehicles to cross the centerline. To hug the edge of the road may invite motorists to try to slip by you when there is insufficient room to do so safely.

- Leave room between yourself and the car in front of you for the motorist to brake.

- Although you may be physically able to ride faster than the going traffic, some situations—like speed limits or traffic jams—demand that you ride the speed of traffic, or slower, for safety. Some riders get impatient. But after all, your frustration is no different than that of drivers of other vehicles who travel slowly in 25-mph zones when they can easily cruise at 65 mph on the highway.

- Sometimes you may have to stop riding and wait for better traffic timing. Consider a road that changes from two lanes plus a shoulder to two lanes without a shoulder going down into a canyon and back up. It may simply not be safe to ride down the hill and be passed by traffic. You may have to wait until a suitable break in traffic allows you to pedal this section of road.

- Sometimes you must avoid certain roads that are just too dangerous to ride, even with proper skills and defensive riding.

INTERSECTIONS

Avoid overtaking vehicles on the inside of the lane, especially buses and trucks at intersections where they may be turning right.

Traveling along Single-lane Roads

To proceed straight ahead: If you are the first to arrive at a red-light intersection, where you stop depends upon the width of the road and what most cars are doing. If most cars will be turning right, for example, stopping in the center of the lane may help make you more visible not only to the car immediately behind you but to following cars as well. It may also allow vehicles turning right to do so unimpeded and with less chance to hit you when they do so.

To make a right turn: Keep to the right, but away from the very edge of the road. Signal before turning, and watch out for other vehicles and pedestrians.

To make a left turn into a minor road: Choose a break in traffic, signal, and move to the middle of the road. If there is no oncoming traffic, make a 90-degree turn into the minor road's right lane. With lots of traffic it is sometimes safer to pull over to the right side of the road and wait for a clear break in traffic before attempting to turn left. Or, turn right, make a U-turn, and wait for a break in traffic or a green traffic light to cross the road.

To make a left turn into a major road: Cross the intersection, going over all of the major road's lanes before turning left. This prevents being trapped in the center of the road by following vehicles.

Traveling along Multiple-lane Roads

To proceed straight ahead: If there is a dedicated right-hand-turn lane, move over to the right of the next (straight-ahead) lane before reaching the intersection.

To make a right turn: Keep to the right, but away from the very edge of the road. Signal before turning; watch out for other vehicles and pedestrians.

To make a left turn: If there is a single dedicated left-turn lane, be on the right side of this lane before turning. If there is a combined turn and straight-ahead lane, it may be impossible to cross this intersection safely from this road. If you are on the left side of the turn lane, you may be trapped in the center of the road onto which you are turning by vehicles also making left-hand turns. If you are on the right of the turn lane you may be prevented from turning by traffic moving straight ahead. Stopping at the intersection may give you a chance to make eye contact with drivers and choose the correct place to ride, possibly the center of the turn lane. Or you may need to make a right turn first, make a U-turn, and wait for a green light or a break in traffic to cross the intersection.

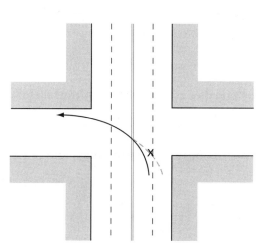

Multiple-lane intersection, turning left: Turn left from the right side of the left-hand lane in a multiple intersection. Avoid crossing traffic lanes at the intersection—get in the proper lane before reaching the light.

SAFETY EQUIPMENT

PROTECTION EQUIPMENT

Always wear a helmet when on a bicycle. Approved helmets can reduce cycling head injuries and death by more than 85 percent. They are lightweight, strong, and ventilated; they fit snugly and have reflective tape. Helmet straps must be in good condition, not frayed, and be adjusted for a snug fit. Once a helmet has been through a crash, it should be replaced. Helmets also improve aerodynamics and make riders faster. Lightweight helmets weigh barely half a pound.

Gloves help protect the hands from injury in case of a fall: an outstretched hand often takes the brunt of a fall. Padded gloves also make riding more comfortable and prevent nerve injuries to the hand.

VISIBILITY EQUIPMENT

Lights are a must at night. Although some headlights are sold with as little as a half watt of light power, many halogen brands with more than 10 watts of power are available. The cost of halogen lights may be higher, but what is the cost of a broken bone, or worse? Movable headlights can be shone in the direction of cross traffic to get the attention of drivers. Rear flashing lights may be more visible than steady ones, and wheel reflectors help drivers at intersections see you. The movement of pedal reflectors also helps you to be seen from behind.

Bright clothing is more visible than dark clothing. Reflective belts or vests improve visibility, especially at night. Flags help draw attention to the bicycle and alert motorists.

OTHER EQUIPMENT

Mirrors help riders see behind them. Just as on cars, mirrors do have blind spots, and looking back is necessary before changing lanes or making abrupt movements.

Bells can help warn pedestrians, but a friendly warning shout can be as effective.

THE ESSENTIAL CYCLIST

4

RIDING

FIRST RIDES

LEARNING HOW TO RIDE?

If you're new to riding, balancing the bicycle may take some practice. Choose a wide road without traffic, or an empty parking lot. I taught my wife to ride when she was thirty-one years old. I had to run along beside her and hold her up just as my dad had to when he first taught me. A safe environment is needed.

If you're new to riding, it may take a while to feel comfortable taking your hands off the handlebars to shift gears, signal traffic, or drink from your water bottle. Take your time and practice—it's something almost all can master.

Quiet roads or parks with wide bike lanes (especially on weekdays) are also good places to ride if you're getting reacquainted with cycling after some time.

For your first rides, don't worry about fancy pedal systems. But even if it's only a ride around the block, get into the habit of always wearing a helmet.

It is true that most people never forget how to ride, though it may take a few outings to remember and feel comfortable again.

BICYCLING CLUBS AND GROUPS

For many, riding with others improves the enjoyment of cycling. Plus, you can learn more about your bicycle from more experienced cyclists.

Almost all cities and towns have bicycling groups. Some are strictly social. Some are for beginners. Some cater mostly to singles. Others are oriented to tandem riding, touring, mountain biking, or racing. Your local newspaper may list local bicycle training rides in its calendar of events. Your area may have specialized bicycling magazines with combined running and cycling calendars. Usually your local bicycle store will be familiar with the local groups and rides. They may advertise local events and races.

PACELINES

Riders training together often work as a group—in a paceline— alternating the lead. After taking a turn riding at the front, in the wind, the lead rider swings off and joins the group at the back of the pack. Riding in the slipstream of others—drafting—is much easier than riding at the same speed solo, since the riders ahead shield you from the wind. At 25 mph, about 20 percent less energy is required riding behind another rider than riding on your own. With more riders, even more energy is saved. Your speed may pick up 5 to 10 mph.

Although beginners sometimes shy away from riding close to one another, it's an easy skill to master. I teach pacelining when coaching the Leukemia Society of America's Team in Training program. My job is to help riders complete 100 miles on a bicycle in a single day. For beginners—well, actually, for almost anyone—that's a long way. But after only a few months of training, we're ready!

One of the techniques that helps us is pacelining. Our teammates share the work, and the effort we each expend individually is reduced. It's almost like having to ride only 75 miles instead of 100.

How Pacelines Work

Imagine five riders riding across the page:

E D C B A

Rider A, finishing a turn at the front, signals and swings to the left, slows down, and rider B takes the lead. Rider A drops in behind rider E:

```
   A           A
 E D C B     E D C B     A E D C B
```

Shortly thereafter, rider B does the same thing:

```
   B           B
 A E D C     A E D C     B A E D C
```

and so on.

GROUP RIDING PRINCIPLES

Certain principles apply when you're riding in a pack of riders. These principles are vital to the safety of the group and its members. Learn them and you'll be welcome in the paceline.

In the beginning, ride with a group of riders at moderate speed. Later, you'll be able to better anticipate what happens when riding in fast packs.

- **No Sudden Moves.** Don't suddenly turn right, left, speed up, or slow down. It is inefficient and dangerous.

- **Be Smooth.** Riders new to pacelines feel the need to show that they can keep up. Some work harder and speed up at the front. This is wrong. The front rider relinquishing the lead moves over to the side and then slows down, slightly. The rider assuming the lead does not speed up, but maintains the same speed.

- **Give Others a Turn.** The idea is not to prove how strong you are by hogging the front, but rather to learn how to work together in a group, ride together, and feel comfortable changing positions. There will be plenty of time to test your strength.

- **Pull Off in a Consistent Direction.** When riding in a group, unless the wind changes, riders will relinquish the lead by "pulling off" either to the left or the right. Whichever way the group is working, pull off the same way.

- **Signal Your Intentions.** When pulling off, the most common signal is to wiggle your elbow on the side of your body that the next rider will come up upon. If you are pulling off to the left and the next rider will come up on your right, wiggle your right elbow. Occasionally a rider will create a gap in the paceline. If you are going to fill it instead of going all the way to the back of the paceline, you can point to the gap and move in.

- **Draft Reasonably Close.** Keep as close to the rider in front of you as you comfortably and safely can. Try to not let "gaps" open.

- **Ride Close Side-to-Side.** When you drop back to rotate, try to ride closely side-to-side as well. This helps to avoid impeding other traffic and is also more efficient because there is less aerodynamic drag when the group is tighter.

- **Warn of Road Hazards.** If there is plenty of time, everyone can avoid the hazard. If there is not much time to avoid some glass or a hole, it is often safer to ride over the hazard than violate Rule #1, *no sudden moves*.

- **Warn of Upcoming Cars.** Large groups sometimes impede the flow of traffic. Riders in the back should warn the group of upcoming cars. The most common shout is "Car back!"

- **Use Brakes as Little as Possible.** Braking wastes the energy you've used building up to speed. It is also dangerous for the rider in back of you.

- **Don't Exhaust Yourself Pulling Too Long.** If you are weaker than the other riders in the group, take the front, but only for a few pedal strokes. Take your turn in front to practice technique and keep the paceline flowing smoothly.

- **Don't Fool with Waterbottles or Food when Leading.** Wait until you've pulled off to eat or drink. Also, try to be in the "right gear" and not change gears when you are leading.

- **Do Not Overlap Wheels.** Ride behind the rider in front of you. With a crosswind, experienced racers ride partially to the side of the rider in front of them to help shield them from the wind. If the rider in front of you moves over slightly, and you are overlapping that back wheel, it is your front end that will be unstable, and it is you who will go down.

- **Stop Signs and Traffic Lights.** Obey the rules of the road. The entire group will be obliged to stop now and then. The front riders should not take off quickly after a stop—there is an accordion effect and the riders at the back have to "catch up."

- **Check Back Occasionally.** Look back occasionally and make sure that you aren't leaving other riders behind.
- **Hills.** Moderate the pace on uphills. As the front rider, don't prove you are the best climber if you want the group to stay together.
- **Downhills.** The front riders must pedal, not coast, or the riders behind will have to use their brakes to avoid running into them.
- **Yells and Screams.** Riders will often yell short commands or advice. These "barks" often seem rude and angry. By and large, no meanness is meant. It is just that there seems to be too little time for full sentences and explanations. Don't take yells and screams personally. Empathize with new riders—avoid yelling and screaming.

COMMUTING

WHY COMMUTE?

For a cyclist, the question is often "How can I afford not to commute?" Here are a few reasons why bicycle commuting makes sense:

- It may take less time than traveling by car and parking.
- It's cheaper.
- It's better for your health—it builds and keeps fitness.
- It's mentally relaxing.
- It's good for the planet.
- You have to get to work anyway. Why not have fun?

Consider starting by riding your bike to work just one or two days a week, then possibly build up to three or four. Most people need a car once or twice a week for errands or appointments.

PARKING YOUR BIKE

An important concern for commuters is what happens to their bikes while they're at the workplace.

The best situation is taking your bike inside, and being able to keep an eye on it. Using an empty closet or storage room in your office can be about as good.

Enclosed bike lockers, in which the bike is secured and invisible to passersby, provide a good measure of safety.

57

Racks in a well-trafficked area usually present some risk of theft. An inexpensive commuter bike may be a better choice to take to work than your two-thousand-dollar racing dream machine.

NEED A SHOWER?

If your commute is less than a few miles in a temperate climate, cleaning up may not be necessary. A rest room and a sponge bath are all that are necessary for most commuters.

If you're lucky, there are showers and lockers at work. Sometimes there's a "hidden" shower on another floor or another section of your building. Ask around. If there is no shower at work, look around for a nearby gym. You may be able to change and shower there, then walk or ride slowly to work. If you want to get a hard workout and there's nowhere to clean up at work, consider making little or no effort riding on the way to work and then getting your workout on the way home.

TOO FAR TO COMMUTE?

If your ride is too long for a round trip consider driving your bike to work and riding home. The next day ride to work and drive home.

Reduce the length of your commute by driving partway and riding the rest of the way or use public transportation to take you some of the way.

If you can carpool, bike racks may allow you to ride one way until it's your turn to drive.

TRANSPORTING WORK CLOTHES AND STUFF

Some bike commuters drive their cars to work once a week with all the clothes they will need for the week. Bike racks and panniers (or saddlebags) or knapsacks allow you to transport papers, food, and clothes. Racks allow you to ride unencumbered by a knapsack and lower your center of gravity, and they come in handy for errands when you don't have your knapsack with you. I use bungee cords to fasten my attaché case to my back rack. My case keeps important documents neat and my sandwiches unsquished.

MAINTAIN YOUR COMMUTING BIKE

It's one thing to ride on the weekend and take 15 minutes longer than planned, but most commuters time their arrival at work fairly tightly—after all, who wants to get there any earlier than necessary?

Keep your bike working well. Learn to fix a flat efficiently. Replace suspect tires. Carry a pump and bring a spare tube, patch kit, and tire irons in a seat bag.

CHOOSING YOUR ROUTE

Here are a few hints to keep in mind when planning your commute:
- Many cities publish maps with suggested bike routes.
- Roads with wide curb lanes are usually safer than narrow roads.
- Bike lanes and multiuse paths (roads shared with bicycles, pedestrians, skaters, horses, and others) may be less safe than the main road because pedestrians, pets, and skaters are unpredictable and require more skill to pass safely. Bicycle path/road intersections can be very dangerous because motorists don't expect vehicular cross traffic.

Although main roads are usually faster and more convenient than side streets, side streets may be a better choice, offering greater safety, less noise, less pollution, and better scenery for those not in a rush.

WHAT TO WEAR AND OTHER ACCESSORIES

The value of cycling clothes on a commute depends on the length of the commute. It is hardly worth commuting 1 mile in cycling clothes and changing to regular clothes at work; 15 miles is a different story.

For very short commutes you can often dress for work. For long commutes, you may want to use cycling shoes and cycling shorts. You'll need a change of shirt, but a cycling jersey is not required. It's easy to leave a pair of shoes at work and carry work clothes in a pannier. Specialized portfolio panniers and knapsacks are available that keep documents neat and work clothes unwrinkled.

Although racers use clipless pedals almost exclusively, toe clips and straps keep your feet on the pedals and can be used with work shoes. They are often a commuter's preference.

Cycling gloves pad the hands, making riding more comfortable and offering some protection if you fall. Long-fingered gloves are needed when the temperature drops. Carry lightweight rain gear when there is any chance of rain. In cold weather, wear layers. A windproof jacket is lightweight and valuable.

Keep reflectors on your commuting bike at all times. It's also a good idea to have a strobing red rear light permanently mounted. Little battery energy is needed, so you'll rarely run out of juice. Protecting your rear is an important safety consideration when riding home from work at night.

Of course, seeing the road ahead means you need a front light at night. More important, cars at intersections will see your headlight. Modern front lights with powerful halogen beams are usually worth the investment if there is even a chance that you will commute in the dark.

COMMUTING AND POLLUTION

Some riders are sensitive to pollution and experience problems such as a worsening of asthma or watery eyes. Here are some strategies for reducing exposure to pollution:

- Ride less-traveled roads. Stop-and-go traffic or busy roads are worse.
- Ride as far as possible to the right, out of the flow of traffic.
- Avoid peak traffic hours.
- Ride in the early morning rather than the late afternoon, when pollution is worse.
- Use sunglasses or clear lenses to protect your eyes.

While it's true that riding in polluted air can be harmful, not riding and not exercising may be worse. Studies show that car commuters are exposed to higher levels of pollution than bicycle commuters.

MOUNTAIN BIKING

The sturdy off-road or mountain bike was developed in northern California in the early 1970s. Joe Breeze and Tom Ritchey were early pioneers. Breeze bought a 1941 Schwinn Excelsior for five dollars in 1973. He'd hitchhike up to the top of Mt. Tamalpais and ride home on the mountain's dirt trails. Gary Fisher fashioned a heavy bike with balloon tires, motorcycle brakes, thumb shifters, adjustable seat height, and wide-range derailleurs. The first mountain bike races were held on a dirt track down Mt. Tamalpais, plunging 1,300 feet in less than 2 miles. The first commercial mountain bikes were available in 1979, and innovation and popularity followed rapidly.

By the 1990s, mountain bikes had become the most popular bikes sold in America. They became lightweight and used suspension for both the front and rear wheels. Some sold for the price of motorcycles.

Mountain bikes made their way into the Olympic Games in 1996. Their national federation, NORBA, had been born barely a decade before, in 1983, when the charter was composed by Breeze and Veloclub Tamalpais buddies in a living room over a few beers. Now NORBA is tens of thousands of members strong and growing.

WHERE ARE MOUNTAIN BIKES RIDDEN?

Although romantic photos of mud-encrusted machines and bodies grace the magazines each month, most people who buy mountain bikes ride them on paved roads. Mountain bikes give a softer, cushier ride than road bicycles. Their upright position may be more comfortable for short rides.

They are not efficient on the road, however—their wider, knobby tires and upright position mean more road and aerodynamic resistance. They are built for paths and trails, and they excel in that environment.

SKILLS

Mountain biking over well-graded dirt fire roads allows you to get away from the hustle and bustle of road traffic. Fire roads present relatively few technical challenges. Many established mountain bike trails, however, are wide enough for only one bicycle at a time—single-track. Sometimes steep descents or ascents, or the presence of gravel or rocks, makes mountain biking an especially skill-demanding sport.

THE MOUNTAIN BIKER'S STRUGGLE

The freedom to travel off-road holds enormous appeal. It holds such great appeal, in fact, that the explosion of the sport has created some problems. Relatively fragile paths have been eroded by the sheer volume of mountain bikes. And hikers, horses, and other trail users seeking peace and quiet are often annoyed by the danger, speed, and noise of mountain bikers.

Although mountain biking can be great for the rider, respect for the other users of the paths is needed to ensure the continued availability of bike trails. Mountain bikers are newcomers to trails—they must prove to be responsible trail users or they will be forbidden access, as has already happened in some areas.

TRAIL RIDING GUIDELINES

Sure you want to have fun on trails. Part of the appeal of trail riding is freedom. Freedom from noise, freedom from traffic, freedom from stoplights and traffic rules. But there are still rules of the road that must be obeyed. Your own safety, the safety of other trail users, and the preservation of the environment demand guidelines. You are sharing the trail with other cyclists, hikers, and horseback riders.

Some of the same rules apply to mountain bikers that apply to all trail users—"Take only pictures, leave only foot or tire prints." Move off the trail to relieve yourself, use only designated campsites, and pack out trash.

In addition:

• Keep your bicycle in excellent operating condition. Be prepared with emergency equipment. You may be miles or hours away from help.

• In remote areas, ride with others, not alone.

• Yield the right of way to nonmotorized trail users. Move off the trail to allow horses to pass and stop to allow hikers adequate room to share the trail.

• Slow down and use caution when approaching other riders. Let others know of your presence well in advance in a friendly way. Simply yelling "bicycle" is often not perceived as friendly.

• Develop your skills. Rocks, gravel and holes make trail riding challenging. Start on easy trails before kamikazeing down tricky descents.

• Maintain control of your speed. Be able to stop safely within the distance you can see down the trail. Approach turns defensively, anticipating someone around the bend.

• Stay on designated trails to avoid trampling vegetation. In some fragile areas, such as desert crust, it takes up to fifty years to recover even from footprints.

- Minimize erosion by not using wet or muddy trails. Don't shortcut switchbacks.

- Avoid wheel lockup. If a trail is steep enough to require locking wheels and skidding, dismount and walk your bike. Locking brakes contributes to needless trail damage.

- Water bars are rock and log drains placed across trails to direct water off the trail and prevent erosion. Ride directly over the top, or dismount and walk your bike.

- Do not disturb wildlife or livestock.

- Respect public and private property, including trail use signs and NO TRESPASSING signs. Leave gates as you found them. If your route crosses private property, obtain permission from the landowner. Don't ride where you are not welcome.

- In National Parks and some other areas, bicycles are considered vehicles and are restricted to roads.

RIDING OFF-DIRT

Off-dirt. That means the road. Love the comfort and feel of your mountain bike? Consider trading your knobby tires for slicks when riding the road. You will still sacrifice a little speed and lightness to road bikes, but you'll enjoy much greater efficiency than with knobby, off-road tires.

TOURING

Bicycle touring—traveling by bicycle for a few days, weeks, or months—offers a unique opportunity to experience the beauty of nature, freedom, and independence. Waking up in one place, packing up the bike, and riding down the road to another brings the cosmos and the country closer to many people, perhaps more than any other means of travel or touring. It fosters personal growth and a feeling of self-confidence.

Bicycle touring takes some preparation. It requires not only fitness but also selecting the right route, time of year, equipment, group of friends, and goals to make a bicycle tour the experience of a lifetime.

Traditional touring has taken place on scenic or less-traveled roadways. Mountain bike touring—on mountain bike trails—is an alternative that is becoming increasingly popular.

PLANNING

Distance

How far you are planning to travel in a day is one of the most important decisions. This is the vital ingredient to your group's compatibility. It's not necessary for everyone to travel at the same speed, but it is necessary for everyone to travel the same distance. Both the weakest rider and the strongest must be comfortable with the distance.

Distances of 50 to 60 miles are typical of many tours. For fit riders, this allows time for stops to view the scenery, meet the local inhabitants, see the sights, write postcards, make camp, and savor meals. Some organized tours in California's wine country plan on only 15 to 20 miles a day, with morning bicycle rides. Afternoons are spent tasting the grape juice.

It is possible to tour 150 or more miles daily. Lon Haldeman, an ultra-distance athlete, organizes cross-country trips lasting just a few weeks.

Accommodations

Camping is the traditional accommodation of bicycle touring. Staying in youth hostels is another. While many enjoy the day-after-day freedom of the outdoors, others prefer the comfort of a motel room, hotel, or local family.

Credit-card touring—eating at restaurants, staying in motels—allows you to reduce the weight of bicycle luggage by more than half. In fact, my wife and I tour the desert in winter with just one change of clothes in our handlebar bags. Of course, neither one of us has ever been accused of being fashionably dressed.

Food

Camp-cooking, eating in restaurants, munching out of grocery stores, or a combination? It's not that one is better than the other. It's a personal preference. But it's something to find out before you agree to join a tour.

Mechanical Problems

Independence is one thing, but you've got to earn it. Of course, if you're part of an organized tour, the tour leaders will be able to help fix just about any mechanical problem. But if you're planning on going with just a small group of friends, you've got to know how to change a flat tire, at a bare minimum. Most seasoned tourers know how to adjust seat height, straighten handlebars, fix broken chains, replace worn brake and gear cables and adjust derailleurs. Carry a patch kit, extra tube, and tools (see page 23).

Injury

It's another responsibility of independence. You should know basic first aid and how to take care of minor cuts, scrapes, and saddle sores. Carry a first-aid kit. For more information on what a first-aid kit should contain, see page 67.

The Route

You'll want to know the terrain, the road conditions, the likely weather conditions, whether construction is interfering with any of the roads, and whether special local events will fill up all the local campsites and motels. It's also useful to have an idea where local bike shops may be located on your route.

The local chamber of commerce, tourist bureau, county or state highway department, and local bike clubs can be valuable resources.

THE GROUP

Almost all groups need a leader. Small groups often make decisions by consensus, and organized tours have everything decided in advance. But there has to be someone empowered to make decisions, an acknowledged leader. Someone who decides, for example, which way to go at the fork in the road and where to camp.

It's not necessary for all riders in a group to ride together at all times.

But it is important to know that the group will get together at certain designated locations, or regrouping points along the way. It's important that those ahead of the group look out for those behind. If those ahead stop to go to the restroom or get something from the store, they should leave their bike, helmet, or something else plainly visible at the side of the road so the riders following can stop and not get ahead. If they do decide to go ahead, those left behind need to know where the others have gone. The group also needs to discuss common group riding principles, such as how to signal road hazards like glass, dogs, or potholes, and how to warn of cars coming up from behind and riders slowing down or stopping.

Group dynamics are important. After several days, small frustrations can build. It's important to have an open and caring attitude toward your companions and be willing to make compromises.

THE BIKE

Touring bikes are sturdy. Their frames are designed to carry heavy loads. Touring bicycle wheels have at least 36 spokes (32 spokes are the norm on road bikes), while 40 spokes in the rear are common.

Touring bikes have fittings for racks, fenders, and multiple water bottles. They're designed for stability and are not as "quick" handling as racing bikes.

Comfort over long distances is important. The frame of a touring bike has "relaxed geometry" for a less jarring ride. Most touring bikes use a traditional drop handlebar. This permits a variety of hand positions. Additionally, the handlebars are padded for comfort.

Mountain bikes are less suitable for road touring, although they are used more and more frequently for that purpose. At a minimum, replace those knobbies with slick, high-pressure mountain bike tires. If your mountain bike has front suspension forks, you won't have the option of attaching front panniers. That means you won't be able to pack as much. Also, the mountain bike handlebar limits hand positions, though bar end attachments can give you more flexibility.

TOURING BAGS

If you are planning on camping and cooking out, you'll probably need front and rear panniers, or saddlebags. Front and rear panniers hold more than 3,000 cubic inches of gear. This is known as fully loaded touring. A handlebar bag will hold immediate essentials, including your map and small snacks.

It's best to balance the weight of your gear between the front and rear bags, and between the left and right sides. Pack heavy objects at the bottom of the bags to keep your center of gravity low.

Although the bag material may be waterproof, seams may leak. Sealing your seams with seam-sealer may help, but no bag is completely waterproof in a downpour. Placing clothing in plastic bags and stowing gear that won't be harmed by water on the top of your bags may help prevent water damage. Waterproof map bags and waterproof containers for some important items will also help.

Panniers affect the handling of your bicycle. Before you go touring, practice riding with your loaded bags. You'll not only learn how to handle the weight but you'll also find out about potential problems—such as inadequate pedal clearance between your heel and the rear bag—before you get off the plane in Timbuktu.

TOOLS

You'll need the basics: Tire irons, tubes, patch kit, Allen keys, slotted and Phillips screwdrivers. Make sure you have the right-size tools to adjust your seat height, seat angle, brakes, and derailleurs. In addition, a replacement foldable tire, cables, chain tool, lubricants, and a 6-inch crescent or vise-grip wrench are required. You may also wish to include freewheel or cassette tools, headset and bottom bracket tools, and an extra chain. If you are traveling in a group, everyone should carry the basics. One person can be the mechanic and carry the heavier or bigger items to share.

FIRST-AID KIT

You'll need the usual—Band-Aids, aspirin or Tylenol, antibacterial ointment, gauze dressings, antihistamines, and personal medications. Knowing first aid is probably more important than having a kit. Read more about first aid or consider taking a first-aid course if you've never taken one.

CLOTHING

Consider the terrain you will be traversing, elevation, wind-chill, and the season.

It's easy to forget, when traveling, that the weather elsewhere is different. Sometimes traveling just 10 miles may place you in a different climate zone. If you travel inland from the ocean to desert, temperatures may rise 1 degree every mile. If you are climbing, temperature may fall a few degrees for every 1,000 feet of elevation gain.

The conventional wisdom on what clothing to take and how to dress is based on layers. On warm days perhaps you'll wear a sleeveless or short-sleeved jersey, cycling shorts, and fingerless gloves. As the weather cools you may want to add a polypropylene T-shirt, long-sleeved jersey, wind jacket, and tights. Thermal socks or shoe covers keep your feet warm. A headband or helmet liner can keep your ears and head toasty. In wet weather, a waterproof jacket, cape, or poncho will keep you dry in mild to moderate rain. In moderate to severe rain, waterproof pants and shoe covers keep the rest of you dry, too.

MISCELLANEOUS ITEMS

In addition to the items discussed above, don't forget:

- Eye protection
- Toiletries
- Bug repellent
- Lip balm
- Sun block
- Towel

- Credit cards
- Cash
- ID
- Camera
- Pocket knife

It's easy to pack too much. Bike touring is not like car touring, for which you can just throw something more in the trunk. When you tour you are carrying every bit of weight up the hill yourself. Most people take too much. Before you actually go touring, pack everything in your panniers and ride up a 2-mile hill. You may find there are lots of items you could have left behind!

THE ESSENTIAL CYCLIST

FOOD

The old adage "Drink before you are thirsty, eat before you are hungry" is still good advice.

A bicycle tour is not the time to plan on losing weight. You need to eat enough to keep your energy stores up day after day. Keep your energy levels high when riding by munching throughout the day. A diet high in complex carbohydrates works best. If it will be some time after your ride before your meal is ready, snack as soon as the ride is over to refuel.

It's impractical to take along all the food you're going to need for the whole trip. Pack along those items that may be hard to find elsewhere—sports bars, mixed nuts and dried fruit, or those staples that you'll want to have handy—peanut butter and jam, for example.

Use local stores for fruits and vegetables. And if you can tolerate skim milk, it's still one of the most wholesome, nutritious products around. Experiment beforehand. Go on rides and see how that new sports bar tastes after you've ridden 30 miles! If camping, it's always a good idea to separate your food from the rest of your belongings and not bring it into your tent with you. In bear country, this may be a vital practice.

There are very few clean streams or lakes. Purifying drinking water is a must. Five drops of iodine per quart or liter of water can help, as can boiling your water or using small pump filters. Freeze-dried food makes camp cooking a no-brainer, and saves time at the local grocery store.

STARTING OUT—THE DEPARTURE POINT

The simplest way is to pack up your panniers and bike and to ride out from home. But clearly, this limits your options on where to ride.

If you are driving to the departure point, are you going to be dropped off or leave your car? If leaving your car, remove your valuables, or at a minimum hide them from view. Of course a secure parking area is best. Often you are starting outside a major city or in the next small town over. Avoid dangerous looking neighborhoods. I've often left my car near a church. Once my wife and I left our car in the parking lot of a condominium complex on the outskirts of Santa Fe, New Mexico, only to find, on our return, that the parking lot had been repaved. Somehow our car was fine, parked on the other side of the buildings!

If you are flying, you'll probably use cardboard boxes to transport your bike. Unless you have a place to store your bike boxes at your destination, you'll have to get new boxes from the airline when you return. Since these boxes are somewhat flimsy, I sometimes stop off at the local hardware store on the way to the airport to get some pipe insulation to wrap around the frame tubes to help protect the bike's paint job. (See more about transporting your bike in chapter 5.)

CAMPING

The Campground

Some campgrounds are quite primitive, with only an outhouse, if that. Others have showers, laundry facilities, stores, swimming pools, and other conveniences. Some campgrounds have hiker/biker sections that are much less expensive than sites for vehicles.

I like to scout out the campground and try to find a relatively quiet and secluded spot, where I won't be awakened by late arrivals. In planning your trip consider contingency options if the campground is too crowded or proves to be too far to ride to. Some may be unavailable without reservations.

The Equipment

Of course you'll need a sleeping bag. Down is still the lightest, most compact insulation, but it's useless when wet. If you're touring the Pacific Northwest, for example, a modern lightweight synthetic might be a better choice, and less expensive, too. A sleeping pad for insulation and comfort is considered a luxury by some, a necessity by others. The most popular pads today are partly foam, partly air-filled.

Your tent should be light and compact. Most have a main body, poles, and a rain fly. Make sure that you have practiced setting it up before you get to your first campsite. When setting up your tent, look for a spot that's level and cleared of debris. If your site has a slight incline, sleep with your head uphill.

Portable stoves are available that are small and lightweight. You'll need a fuel bottle for storing extra fuel. Store these items in leakproof bags in a separate section of your panniers.

I still marvel when I read that you need waterproof matches in a waterproof container. Forget them. Just buy a cheap lighter.

Securing Your Bike

There's a risk that your bike may be stolen while you're sleeping. Securing the bike with a lock to your tent or an immovable object such as a tree is a good idea. Alternatives are stowing your front wheel in your tent with you or otherwise temporarily disabling your bike.

HILLS

Hills, while you're riding fully loaded, present a unique challenge. On flat land you can ease up a lot and still make significant progress. But on hills resting means getting off the bike. So it's important to find your own rhythm and pace. Remember, hill climbing is not a race, so be prudent and keep your pace moderate and conserve energy. Relax as you climb and change positions. Shift to a slightly harder gear and stand every once in a while to get the pressure off your rear end.

If you do decide to rest and get off your bike, don't let it be for more than 5 or 10 minutes—it's hard to get going again on an incline. Focusing on breathing helps many people keep their concentration and get to the top. Mentally divide the climb into sections, and focus on completing each section, rather than looking at how far away the crest of the hill is.

You'll find you can descend a lot faster with all that added weight. Feather your brakes. Keep your speed under control. A common touring problem is a front-end shimmy that occurs when going downhill. Usually the problem is too much weight in the rear panniers, although the usual contributing causes—loose headset or misaligned frame—are amplified with loaded touring.

SAFETY

The common important issues of bicycle safety apply to bicycle touring:

- Mechanically safe bicycle equipment. It's especially important to check tires, brakes, and cables daily when touring.
- Skills and techniques. Riding safely includes knowing how to deal with common road hazards; such as narrow shoulders, potholes,

gravel, cattle guard grates, railroad crossings, dogs, traffic, tunnels, and reflector buttons.

- Defensive riding. All the defensive riding techniques described in chapter 3 apply. Logging trucks are sometimes feared by touring riders, but it's the campers and RVs driven by nonprofessional drivers that are most likely to come too close.
- Safety equipment. Safety equipment includes helmet, mirror, and bright clothing and reflective strips on bags. Riding at night? It's prudent to fit a rear-mounted flashing light in case you end up cycling a little later than you figured; a bright front light is required if nighttime riding is in your plans. You can read more about safety in chapter 3.

STAYING COMFORTABLE

The right, well-maintained bike helps, as do the right clothes. Frequent short rests also prevent potential aches and pains.

When selecting your saddle, go for comfort, not necessarily for the lightest weight. A seat pad can help if the built-in padding isn't enough.

Stretch and relax on and off the bike. When standing, let one heel drop down to stretch your calf. Vary the position of your hands. While riding, wriggle your fingers and shoulders. Consciously relax your elbows and back. Stand occasionally while climbing. Don't focus just on one spot on the road—turn your head side-to-side and enjoy the view.

RIDING A CENTURY

One hundred is a very round number. Riding a century means riding 100 miles. (Occasionally riders "cheat" and ride a metric century—100 kilometers, about 62 miles.) The challenge of riding 100 miles in one day holds great appeal to many riders.

Can you ride a century? Almost certainly—if you set your mind to it, train properly, and follow a few simple tips.

Events are organized throughout the country to help cyclists ride 100 miles in one day, though, of course, it's possible to do it on your own. What the event organizers do is specify a starting time and provide a starting place, rest stops with food and drink along the way, emergency services, and a finish area, usually with a lot of food—perhaps a band or other entertainment, commemorative certificates, patches or T-shirts. In short, they really create an event.

As part of fund-raising to discover a cure for leukemia and other related diseases, I've helped the Leukemia Society of America run three- to six-month training programs for cyclists. These programs enable beginning riders to finish 100 miles in one day and help raise money to fight leukemia. Many of these riders have a deep commitment to raising money—some of them are much more interested in the charity than in riding. Some of these riders start with barely serviceable bikes, hardly know how to shift gears, and have never ridden more than a few miles in a single day. Some of them are senior citizens.

But with commitment, they build up to riding a century in six months or less. I've shown some of them how to do it. If they can do it, so can you.

If a century is something you want to do, here are some tips on how.

TARGET YOUR EVENT

Wanting to ride a century is a specific goal. But you've got to focus even more. When are you going to ride that century?

Perhaps you'll choose a local event—and local bike stores or cycling groups will be able to help you pick a day. Or perhaps you'll go on a little vacation across the state, or across the country, to participate in one of the better-known centuries that attract thousands of participants. A number of bicycling magazines list these events, or the League of American Bicyclists (see appendix A, For More Information) may help you find one.

FINISH OR RACE?

Is your goal to finish your first century, improve a past century time or performance, or to stay with the lead riders and race?

The goal for most riders is to finish. Centuries are not licensed races, they are fun rides. Although many riders like to improve their times from past events, keep in mind that there are often stop signs, traffic lights, and crowds that limit your speed. You must not sacrifice safety and courtesy to gain a few minutes. And you can't really compare times from one century to another, because of hills, winds, and other differences.

Although a decade ago most centuries started all participants at the same time, nowadays more centuries start riders in small groups or waves. These are definitely not races. After all, how can they be when some riders have started 30 minutes ahead of others?

However, there are still some race-centuries, which allow racers to start at the head of the bunch. These centuries may provide official finishing times, but most do not.

WATCH OUT FOR TOUGH CENTURIES

Experienced century riders may revel in a challenge. They sometimes look for the hilliest, toughest centuries. It's common for difficult centuries to brag how hard they are with names such as Killer, Death Ride, or Challenge in their title. Watch out!

SET A TRAINING SCHEDULE

If you are relatively new to cycling, plan on training for four to six months. If you are an experienced rider, perhaps only a few months are needed. A typical program is provided on the next page.

ORGANIZE YOUR TRAINING WEEK

Most of us have a lot more time to train on the weekends than during the week. To train properly, we need one long ride a week. I prefer to schedule that ride for Saturday. If rain or something else prevents me from riding, I always have Sunday to fall back on. Plan on riding three days a week at the beginning of your program. The last three months of training, try to ride five days a week.

VARY YOUR WORKOUTS

Nothing kills enthusiasm more than unvarying repetition—the same ride at the same pace all the time. Sure, you might plan long rides at a steady pace. And you may have to work a little harder climbing hills. Your other rides can be spiced up with extra-hard efforts (or intervals) and look-at-the-flowers or do-errands easy days.

DEALING WITH RAIN OR DARKNESS

If your schedule calls for training on a bad-weather day, or work prevents you from riding during the day, you still have a few choices. You can dress for the weather. You can use a lighting system—some of the new ones, though expensive, seem almost as bright as car headlights. Riding in rain or darkness usually means you should slow down for safety.

You can ride a Lifecycle or stationary trainer. Stationary trainer devices allow you to mount your bicycle and stay in one spot that is dry, well lit, and warm. Riding a stationary trainer usually means you need to have a workout program in mind before you get on the trainer—or going nowhere becomes old, fast. Stationary trainer workouts are discussed more in chapter 6.

CENTURY TRAINING PROGRAM

Here's a typical five-month training program for a new rider. Riders looking to improve their times could add 10 percent to the weekly mileage. Racers add 25 percent.

A. Building a Base—The First 10 Weeks

Week Intensity	Mon	Tue	Wed =	Thu	Fri	Sat = or +	Sun −	Weekly Mileage
1			7			18	10	35
2			8			20	12	40
3			10			25	15	50
4			12			30	18	60
5			11			28	16	55
6			12			30	18	60
7			14			35	21	70
8			12			30	18	60
9			14			35	21	70
10			15			38	22	75

Riding Intensity Definitions:

(=) Pace: The speed you wish to maintain during the century.

(−) Below pace: Easier than you plan to ride during the century. Riding so that you are breathing normally. It's quite leisurely. If you use a heart-rate monitor, it's under 65 percent of your heart rate.

(+) Above pace: Harder than you plan to ride during the century. Riding a few miles an hour faster than your century pace, or interval work.

During the program, your long ride is scheduled for Saturday. Since

RIDING

the ride may be with friends, you'll probably find yourself riding hard as well as long. Ride only about half the distance on Sunday, and ride easy.

Try to ride one day during the week as well. Build up to about 15 miles, or up to 1 to 1.5 hours of riding time.

B. Building Up—The Last 10 Weeks

Week Intensity	Mon	Tue +	Wed =	Thu	Fri −	Sat = or +	Sun −	Weekly Mileage
1		5	20		5	45	15	90
2		10	25		5	50	15	105
3		10	30		5	45	20	110
4		10	30		5	50	20	115
5		15	30		5	60	25	135
6		15	30		5	70	25	145
7		15	30		10	70	30	155
8		15	30		10	75	30	160
9		15	30		10	80	30	165
Century Week		20	30		5	5	100	160

For the last ten weeks ride five days a week. Increase your long Saturday ride up to a maximum of 80 miles. Experienced century riders and racers will do more. Sunday remains a recovery or easy ride at about half Saturday's distance.

Overview	First 10 Weeks	Second 10 Weeks
Mondays	Off	Off
Tuesdays	Off	Above pace
Wednesdays	Pace	Pace; medium distance
Thursdays	Off	Off
Fridays	Off	Below pace
Saturdays	Pace, or above	Pace, or above; long distance
Sundays	Below pace	Below pace

Ride a few miles on Fridays, to loosen up for the weekend and make sure that your bike is working perfectly. If you have a problem with your bike, you can afford to bag the Friday ride and get a quick fix at home or at the bike shop. You don't want any problems getting in the way of your longer weekend rides.

Ride two other days in the middle of the week. I've scheduled Tuesday and Wednesday. It could be Wednesday and Thursday, or any other combination of days. By placing those rides in the early part of the week you've got Thursday to fall back on in case Tuesday or Wednesday doesn't work out. During the shorter of the two, in our case Tuesday, ride extra hard up hills, or do intervals or something else to make this shorter ride more intense.

Notice how the last week, the week of your century, your total mileage for the week is a little less than that of the week before. Your body is ready—you can do it!

TIPS FOR YOUR CENTURY RIDE

Riding 100 miles in one day is a terrific challenge—and a landmark event in the career of any cyclist. Here are some tips to make your training and century event easier and more fun.

New Gear

Don't try new gear during your event. Bike equipment, clothing, food, sports drinks: Test and make sure things work well in training.

Hydrate

Prehydrate and drink often while you ride. Carry two water bottles. (Have extra fluids in your car for when you return from training rides. Cool fluids go down more easily.) Drink before you are thirsty. Drink some calories while you're at it: perhaps half-strength fruit juice, Gatorade—whatever you've tried before that works for you. Lost fluids decrease performance. Dehydration increases heat stress and hyperthermia.

Calories

The century will use up a lot of calories—at least 2,500. You need to eat before you ride (have a good breakfast). You need to eat while you ride, and during rest stops along the way. Try to eat 300 to 500 calories per hour. Fig bars, bananas, bagels, energy bars, carbohydrate gels. They all work as energy sources. As stated above, try foods before your event

RIDING

to see what you like and make sure they agree with you. (Have extra food in your car for when you return from long training rides.)

Change Positions

Don't get locked into the same position. Stand up, shrug your shoulders, move your arms, wiggle your fingers and toes. Stretch and relax on the bike.

Maps and Directions

Read over your training or century route before you start riding. Carry maps with you.

Find a Group to Ride with, Draft Efficiently

Riding in the slipstream of others at speed often reduces the work by about 25 percent. Find the right group to help you keep your average speed faster than you could accomplish alone. Riding with a group is also less mentally fatiguing, and helps the time pass more easily.

Be Prepared

You need a spare tube, tire irons, patch kit, pump, and Allen keys. Know how to use them.

Get Padded

Protect your rear end and hands. Padded cycling shorts, handlebar tape, and gloves work.

Bring the Right Clothes

Test and break in your clothing. Be prepared for cold weather or rain. A lightweight wind or rain jacket is often a good idea. Always pack a big garbage bag, which can be used as an emergency rain poncho, in your travel bag. You don't need to bring it on the ride if the weather is perfect, but it's nice to have it in case you need it. If traveling to the mountains or other possibly cold areas, long-fingered gloves and tights or leg warmers can be useful.

It's okay to be slightly cool at the start—that way you won't have to start disrobing 10 minutes into the ride.

Wear Sunscreen

Of course it protects your skin. It can also prevent you from getting overheated and can keep you working longer.

Get a Tune-Up

Have your bike working perfectly the week before your event, and check it out again the day before. A clean, lubed, efficient drive train makes you faster. Properly inflated tires are a must.

Rest a Little If You Need To

If you need a breather and to sit down for a few minutes, that's fine. But don't sit around too long, or stiffness and lack of motivation may overcome you.

Use Fast Wheels

Sure you can do a century on a mountain bike with knobbies. But slick, high-pressure tires will improve any bike's speed. Aerodynamic wheels (with fewer than the standard number of spokes) will also help. A road bike, built for speed, will outperform a mountain bike or hybrid.

Consider Aerobars

Aerodynamic handlebars come in various shapes. Most allow you to rest your elbows or forearms on the bar and bring your arms together to decrease aerodynamic resistance. On long-distance rides they provide another handlebar position to increase comfort. They make you faster but make bike handling more difficult, so practice using them before your event. Use them when riding solo or at the head of a group, but not within packs when you need maximum control.

Train Right

Build up your mileage systematically and progressively. Increase mileage no more than 10 to 15 percent weekly. Plan to allow for proper rest and recovery. Taper slightly before your event.

Train for Speed

Ride 10 percent of your weekly mileage above event-pace.

Watch the Climbs

Pushing on the climbs in training will make you stronger. Stronger riders: Pushing a little on the climbs in the event will improve your overall time. Weaker riders: Be conservative when climbing. Save your energy—you've got a long way to go.

Pace Yourself

Don't go out too fast. Too much early enthusiasm can lead to exhaustion later in the day. Know your limits.

Breathing

It's something almost every coach knows, but too few of us practice. Concentrate on your breathing, get a rhythm coordinated with your pedal stroke, and you'll go faster.

Consider Caffeine

A little caffeine before and during the ride may help delay fatigue and keep you going. (As a diuretic, caffeine may also cause you to drink more and stop more often to urinate.)

Think Positive

Motivation improves performance. Focus on your goals, train properly, and go to your event with confidence. Look at the century as ten 10-mile rides. By breaking it down into sections, it's less overwhelming. If you can get a cheering group positioned at the halfway point, it may provide a morale boost. Plan on a reward at the end of the ride, and focus on it if the going gets tough near the end.

Keep It Fun

You're doing this for fun. It's not a job. Avoid placing too many demands on yourself. Keep your perspective. Concentrate on what you can do, not what you can't.

Keep It Safe

As mentioned above, a week or two before the century get your bike a tune-up and make sure it's in tip-top shape. After traveling, equipment sometimes needs adjustment. Ride at least half an hour, with a few hard efforts, the day before your century, to make sure everything is working properly.

Wear a helmet and gloves. Pay attention to the road. Ride straight. Don't cut people off, and don't shave fractions of a second by cutting corners too fast. Don't ride over your skill level, putting yourself in dangerous situations. And don't get so excited by the event that you forget everyday safety rules, such as stopping at stop signs or traffic lights.

RACING

Bicycle racing is fast and exciting, and it brings fitness to an entirely new level. I first began riding as a commuter in Montreal, traveling 2 miles back and forth to college. When I immigrated to San Diego, I began riding more for fitness and fun most weekends. I went to a few local races, but never thought I'd ever race. I watched events on the local roadways as well as on the track, or velodrome. As I became stronger, I tried road racing. A few years later I got up the courage to try track racing.

Surprisingly, it was a lot easier to start than I'd expected. My club teammates helped me, and I went further in the sport than I would have ever thought possible.

I began coaching my teammates after several years of racing. Time and time again I found that ordinary riders could become national-level racers. My group, a local club, has produced dozens of National Champions and U.S. record-holders—more than any other club in the country. I don't believe our riders are genetically gifted. I think that, like me, they dare to dream. Importantly, they put in the time and train. And for those without a lot of time, they train intelligently.

This chapter will enumerate the different types of bicycle races and give information for the aspiring racer.

TYPES OF BICYCLE RACES

The most well known are the Olympic-type races: those held on roadways (road races), those on specialized tracks, or velodromes, and those off the road (mountain bike races).

USA Cycling is the national governing body for most bicycle racing in the United States. It oversees the USCF (United States Cycling Federation), the U.S. amateur national governing body for road and track racing; Pro Cycling, the U.S. professional national governing body for road and track cycling; and NORBA (National Off-Road Bicycle Association), the U.S. national governing body of mountain bike racing.

Other types of races include BMX (bicycle moto-cross), mostly for younger riders; endurance events such as RAAM (the Race Across AMerica); and HPV (human powered vehicle) races, in which bicycles may use fairings.

Racings may be individual competitions against the clock for time, called time trials, or events in which many riders start together, called mass start races.

Road Races

There are three categories: time trials, criteriums, and road races.

Time trials are races against the clock. Riders are started at 30- to 60-second intervals and each rides alone over a set distance for time. Such races are typically held for 10 miles at the local level, or 40K (a little under 25 miles) at the state or national level.

Criteriums are races on circuits up to a mile in length, often with many corners and frequently on flat terrain. These races involve specific racing skills such as cornering and riding together in close groups (packs). The ability to quickly surge and respond to differences in speed is important in these events.

Road races are typically held over smaller state highways or partially closed urban routes. These are more like the rides most beginning cyclists may be familiar with, only at high speed.

Track Races

There are many different types of track races. The traditional championship events are sprints, points races, and time trial-like events over distances of 1, 3, or 4 kilometers (about 0.5 to about 2.5 miles). Weekly local velodrome racing has many more types of mass-start race formats than can be listed here. Here are a few:

Sprint competitions are usually held over distances of about half a mile. Two or three riders participate at a time. Because of the effect of the slipstream, the sprint often does not begin in earnest until only 200 meters (yards) are left in the race!

Points races are races over many laps—say 50—with mini competitions, say every 5 laps. Points are awarded to the four lead riders of each mini competition. Final placings are determined from the overall winners of the mini races.

Kilos, or 1-kilometer time trials, are individual races for that distance on the track.

Pursuits are races of 3 or 4 kilometers. This once-on-one competition is an event with two opponents on opposite sides of the track, performed in heats. In Masters racing, a race of this distance is usually a time trial—an individual effort for time.

Mountain Biking

This is the fastest-growing type of racing. More mountain bikes are now sold than any other type of bicycle. Although traditional road racing is still popular worldwide, mountain biking may be the wave of the future.

There are several types of races for mountain bikes:

Cross country is what most people think of when they think of a mountain bike race. This is a race over dirt trails, usually with a mix of hill climbing, descending, and level riding. Sometimes the trail provides room for only one bike at a time—single track.

Downhill, as the name suggests, means getting down a hill as fast as possible. Technical skill is critical.

Dual slalom is a downhill event similar to skiing. Racing down a hill against another rider provides the excitement of seeing both competitors at the same time.

Trials are a specialized form of mountain biking—balancing and overcoming physical obstacles such as logs. Skill, rather than fitness, is the key.

RACING CATEGORIES

Racers are grouped or classed by age, sex, and ability.

Age and Sex Categories

Divisions may vary slightly, but, in general, Juniors are eighteen years of age and under. Espoirs are under twenty-three. Masters are thirty and over. Women usually race separately, sometimes all lumped into one group.

Ability Categories, Upgrading Procedures

Racers are categorized by experience and talent. In USCF racing there are five categories for amateur male riders, four for females. Men begin as Category 5 riders, women as Category 4. Category 1 is the top level of amateur rider.

A point system assigns points based on placing, with more points being given for higher placings. A certain number of points makes it possible or necessary to upgrade.

Masters

About half of all racers in the United States are Masters. The Masters category starts at age thirty, but the event promoter may choose to have a race for any age group—for example, those over thirty-five or forty-five. At national-level events, the age categories may be as narrow as five years—all the way up to the oldest rider, perhaps an eighty-year-old.

You can race by age if you are a Masters racer, or by category. If you are a forty-three-year-old man, it may be more fun and safer to race with the over-forty-year-olds. But you may have to race with all over-forty-year-olds, who may include some Cat 3 and 2 riders, and occasionally a Cat 1 rider. Or you may choose to race with the Cat 5s, without age restriction. Or you may race both!

Women

Women always have the prerogative to race with men, but not vice versa. Some choose to race with men in order to train at a higher level.

Masters women may race with Masters men up to twenty years older than they are.

Start with Time Trials

Few special skills are required to race by yourself against the clock. For this reason road time trials are a good way to see how you are doing and to assess your prospects for racing with others (mass start races).

Men nineteen to thirty-nine: If you can ride 10 miles in under 30 minutes, you may be ready for some mass start races. Women, older Masters, and Juniors: Add a couple of minutes.

MASS START RACES

Bicycling is a lot different from jogging or running. Whereas anyone can go out and run, bicycle racing involves considerably more skills.

If you go out to run a 10K, chances are that some runners will be a lot slower and some a lot faster. You can continue to train on your own, and strive to improve your personal 10K time. When you start a bicycle road race with others, however, a prerequisite level of ability is required, because you must be able to stay with the main group of riders (the pack). Without the benefit of the pack's slipstream to break air resistance, you are out of the race. The slipstream is much less important in most mountain biking, where speeds are slower. There, skill and time-trialing ability are more important.

Most races require you to have a racing license, though you may occasionally see a race advertised as a public or citizen race, for which a license is not required. This might be a place to start, but such races are infrequent. Your club may have training races for beginners.

RACING CLUBS

USCF bicycle clubs offer much more than just rides to help you develop as a racer. Look for a bicycling club oriented toward racing. In many cities, several choices may be available. If you are a Masters rider, seek a club with a Masters group. Juniors should look for juniors programs, and women for clubs that have a special interest in their development.

Most clubs will allow you to ride with them for several weeks at no charge. This will be a good time to assess your abilities and to determine whether the club is suitable for you. If you enjoy riding with a club, you can usually join for about thirty-five dollars. There is no need to obtain a racing license to join a club.

Clubs Teach Skills

Ideally, the club you have selected will have a beginner's group, in which experienced racers and coaches will show you the ropes and teach racing safety and skills. Once you start riding with a group, you will learn about many things you really did not need to know when riding on your own: things like how to follow another rider closely—to expend less effort—and also ride safely at the same time. Things like how to turn a corner without loss of speed, or how to suddenly and explosively accelerate your bicycle. These skills are required in racing, but not in solo riding.

Racing for Newcomers

Most clubs have training or development races, in which you can ease your way into a race atmosphere without formally entering a licensed race. Such training races will give you a good idea of what is required to race. You can compare yourself with the already established racers and find out at what level you are riding.

YOUR FIRST RACE

You've decided to enter your first race. Here are some of the basics you'll need to know to let you concentrate on racing!

Rule Book

Like any sport, cycling has rules and regulations to ensure fair competition and the safety of the participants. When you join USA Cycling, whether the USCF or NORBA, you'll receive a rule book. When you receive it, review it thoroughly.

Where to Find out about Races

When you join the USCF or NORBA, you receive a monthly magazine about racing. This magazine lists important national races, but it probably won't help you find local races.

Many states have local racing associations that publish listings of all races in the state. Contact your state representative to inquire about local races. Your state rep's name and telephone number are in the back of the rule book. Ask your local bicycling racing club how to find out about local races.

Your First Course

For your first races, choose a course without many sharp turns, and without too many challenging hills. In that way you will more likely be able to stay with the group and finish. As you see how you do, and judge your skills, you know better when to enter more challenging races.

After racing a few times, you'll want even more information on the specifics of training, intervals, sprint workouts, and the like. Though often such information is available from books, your club will be in the best position to help you.

Arriving at Your First Race

Plan on arriving at least an hour before your race is scheduled to start. Although races do run behind schedule, "They are always on time when you are late."

You'll need time to get your numbers, locate the course, and warm up. For some events, riders warm up for over an hour. Locate the registration table. There may be a separate, shorter line for those who have preregistered. Everyone must have a racing license to race.

Determine from the officials present whether the race is running on schedule. Check where numbers are to be placed, and pick up some safety pins. It's a good idea to have extra pins in your race bag—the promoter occasionally runs out. Locate the toilets, for present or future use.

It's your responsibility to know the course. You'll want to be especially aware of the starting and finishing areas. For some races, you'll want to scout out the race before race day.

Riders are usually called to the line at the start of a race. Occasionally they are called to a separate staging area before promenading to the start line. Determine if your race has a separate staging area.

Check Your Equipment

Make sure your bicycle is in tip-top shape before you race. You are responsible for dangerous equipment and risk sanction if poor maintenance or faulty equipment causes a crash. Pumps and road kit bags should not be on a bicycle in a criterium.

Checking Race Results

The number of places to be awarded is announced before the start of the race. In an extremely small field, only one rider—the winner—may be recognized. Occasionally fifty riders in a large, national-level competition may be placed. In Category 3, 4, and 5 racing, five to ten places are normally awarded.

Finished your race and think you've placed? Well, maybe you have, and maybe you haven't. In the rush for the line, adrenaline clouds judgment; you may be mistaken as to where you finished. Sometimes the officials may not be able to place you. If your number was positioned so it could not be read, you may be omitted from the placings. Anyone can make a mistake, so check the official results.

In races that are easy to score, results may be posted in just a few minutes. In others, in which a photofinish requires close examination of a photograph, or when many races are being held simultaneously, or when all participants' finishing times must be individually recorded, results can take hours. Once results are posted, you have 15 minutes to protest an error. After 15 minutes, the posted results become official.

After Your Race

Drink a bottle or two of fluid after your race—you are almost certainly dehydrated. Eat something too—replacing a couple of hundred calories of carbohydrates helps to refuel your energy supplies.

In almost every race some things go well, others less than optimally. Consider factors other than your time and whether you placed. Did you perform well? What would you do differently next time? Consider how you might improve.

Don't whine to others about how you might have done better, how equipment problems prevented your win, how other riders teamed up against you, or how it "wasn't your fault" you didn't do better. If you have a legitimate beef, protest quietly.

Wear your current club jersey to the awards area if you placed. Give appropriate credit to others for your successes. Promoting a race takes a lot of time and energy. Make it a habit to thank at least one person—whether the promoter, a local sponsor, or corner-marshal volunteer—every race.

RACING RECIPE

Many riders think that all you need to be a good racer is strength. Racing is more complicated than that. Here are the ingredients to successful racing:

- Fitness
- Strategy and tactics
- Position on the bicycle
- Bicycle specs and maintenance
- Bike handling
- Psychological state
- Rest, recovery, and sleep
- Body composition
- Physical health
- Diet and ergogenics

Successful Racing

Consider each of the above ingredients. Try to optimize each one. Successful racing and training are discussed in great detail in my book *Smart Cycling* (see appendix A, For More Information).

STATIONARY TRAINING

Stationary training is riding a bicycle in place. It may be on a Lifecycle or Spinner machine in a gym, or it may be on your own bicycle mounted on a special support.

Many people think of riding stationary trainers when the weather is cold or rainy, or when they are on vacation, to keep cycling fitness, in their hotel gym.

Some benefits of stationary trainers are difficult to obtain in any other way. There is value in trainer workouts all year round.

For most people, riding a trainer is a solitary experience, but it need not be that way. Consider forming a stationary trainer group and training together. Trainers allow faster riders to ride with slower ones. I've been running stationary trainer workouts for the last ten years. This winter I expect 150 riders a week to train with me on my patio!

STATIONARY TRAINER ADVANTAGES

- It's fun.
- It's time efficient.
- It's convenient.
- It's relatively inexpensive.
- It's good in the rain and at night.
- It promotes fitness.
- It can offer a hard workout.
- It's a bicycling-specific workout.
- It's motivating.
- It can be social, too.

WHAT TYPE OF TRAINER SHOULD I BUY?
Use a Conventional Stationary Trainer

Get an old-style conventional trainer, one on which you mount your bike after taking off the front wheel, or a "track-stand"-type trainer, one on which your rear wheel is cradled and your front wheel is left on. Conventional trainers are more stable but less portable than "track stand" trainers.

Lifecycle or Spinner machines are great to use when on vacation. But they do not mimic the "feel" of road resistance as closely as the much less expensive conventional trainers, which allow you to use your own bicycle. And your own bicycle is always set up for you—with correct bike fit, the pedals you're used to, and the seat to which you're accustomed.

Resistance

You'll need some resistance device, fan, fluid, or resistance created magnetically or electronically. Fans are the cheapest but noisiest option.

In my experience, magnetic-resistance trainers perform imperfectly. The "magnet" seems lumpy. As effort and cadence increase the magnetic resistance does not vary, so you don't get the right "road feel." Fluid-resistance trainers have a better road feel than mags, but I still prefer fan resistance.

Quiet—the real advantage of mag and fluid trainers—isn't enough to offset the disadvantages. Get a fan-resistance device.

Electronic Trainers

Technology is developing. CompuTrainer's thousand-dollar trainer provides power (watts) output, along with an interactive computer video display. These are valuable tools. Preprogrammed courses motivate some riders. But this trainer doesn't have good road feel and is "lumpy" at low cadences.

STATIONARY TRAINER HINTS
Use an Old Bike

Without the bike moving freely underneath you, enormous pressures are generated on the bicycle. The bike you use on the trainer gets wet with sweat and rusts in time. The headset, with the bike always "going" straight ahead, gets grooved. For these and many other good reasons, if you are a regular stationary trainer enthusiast, don't use an expensive bike. Any old or used bike will do, just make sure it is set up identically to your regular bike.

Gearing

Although almost any gear setup can be made to work, the type of cog setup that has worked best for most of my riders is a 12-13-14-15-16-17-20-28. The closely spaced high gears allow you to tune the hard efforts precisely. The large 28-cog allows you to work on spin and leg speed without muscle strength or aerobic capacity limiting the drill.

Fans for Cooling

Set up two large fans to help evaporate perspiration and to prevent dripping sweat. You'll work harder and longer with them.

Computer with Cadence, Heart-Rate Monitor

Specific workout plans demand a cadence computer, which allows you to tune your efforts precisely, see your progress, and record your improvement. A heart-rate monitor also gives you important feedback about your workout.

DEMO STATIONARY TRAINER WORKOUT

Workout Plan

The secret of falling in love with stationary training is to have a plan, a goal.

Many people find it hard to ride trainers for more than 20 to 30 minutes. Those bored with stationary training usually ride at the same speed and in the same gear for all of their workouts. Challenging variation is required. This fall I trained fifty beginners to ride the 111-mile Tour of Tucson to help raise money for the Leukemia Society of America. With the fall time change, most had difficulty riding during the week. I had riders train 2 hours on stationary trainers on my patio. These riders loved the workouts. If those novices can ride 2 hours, so can you!

Here's a typical workout. Between each exercise is an easy-pedaling rest period.

Duration	Exercise	Gear	RPM	Intervals
10 minutes	Warm-up	39/21	to 120	
20 minutes	Isolated leg	53/17	50 to 60	4- and 3-minute reps
10 minutes	Hill climbing	53/14	50 to 60	
25 minutes	Progressive	53/16	80	two 9-minute reps
20 minutes	30-second intervals	53/16	100+	eight 30-second reps
10 minutes	Cool-down	39/21	100	

Workout Basics

Different aspects of these fitness parts are emphasized during different parts of the workout.

Gears and cadences are meant to be examples only. Rider fitness, types of trainer, and trainer setup all affect power output and make predetermined gear-selection impossible.

Warm-up, Spin-up

The first 10 minutes are spent warming up. Choose the easiest, or almost easiest gear, available. Start at about 60 rpm—that is, pedaling one stroke every second. Build up 5 rpm every minute until you are spinning about 120 rpm. If you are new to cycling, it may take some time to be able to spin this quickly.

Isolated Leg Training

One of the best ways to work on leg strength is one leg at a time. By pedaling with just one leg—isolating that leg—you can focus on pulling up, on evenly applying force to the pedals around the stroke, and on building tremendous push-down forces. The key is to focus on the leg, not the cardiovascular system—which is precisely what ILT does. You can rest your nonworking leg on the back of the trainer, or uses boxes or other objects to support it.

An easy gear will force you to concentrate on smoothness and the pulling up motion of your leg. A hard gear will, in addition, specifically strengthen your quads and gluts—the most important cycling propulsive muscles you have.

Hill Climbing

Place a 4 x 4 block of wood, perhaps 24 inches long, under the front of your trainer. Choose a very hard gear. Stand up and pedal 50 to 60 rpm.

Build up to standing for 10 minutes. You'll feel more confident and you'll be stronger at getting over real hills when you meet them.

Progressive Intervals

Here's a favorite. Choose a moderate gear and pedal at an efficient 80 rpm for 3 minutes. Choose a gear that's hard enough so that at the end of these 3 minutes your heart rate is about 75 percent of your max, perhaps 140 to 150 beats per minute—too fast to carry on a conversation comfortably.

After 3 minutes, shift to the next harder gear and keep riding at the same cadence. At the end of these 3 minutes you'll be working very hard.

Then try one more 3-minute interval in yet another, harder gear. At the end of this 3-minute interval you should be gasping and your legs should be heavy. Another minute or two of work, without recovery, should not be possible.

Repeat this 9-minute exercise.

Short Group Intervals

Four people make this next exercise fun, although you can do it alone. For large groups, do it with the group divided into four sections. When you have a trainer class of fifty riders, each section with a dozen riders, it's great fun!

In turn each rider, or section, pedals as hard as possible in a moderately hard gear at 100 to 140 rpm for 30 seconds. Everyone else pedals easily at the same time. When the 30 seconds are up, the next rider or section takes over. The 30-second intervals progress through the riders until, after a rest of 90 seconds, it's up to the initial rider or section to start pedaling hard again. Try for eight 30-second intervals.

Cool-down

Almost as important as the warm-up and the work itself is a proper cool-down. Spin your easy gear up to 100 rpm, hold it for 4 or 5 minutes, and gradually spin down. I always remember the racehorse adage. By the time it gets back to the barn after a hard workout, it should be breathing normally and not sweating.

5

TRAVEL WITH
YOUR BICYCLE

BY CAR

WITHOUT RACKS

Many of my friends buy minivans for their bicycles. The bike just wheels into the vehicle. But it always seems like a lot more car than I need.

I've always bought hatchbacks. My Mazda 323 cost under eight thousand dollars new. By removing their front wheels, I can put two single bicycles in the back of it and shut the hatchback door without any problem. Leaving the hatchback open, I can even add a tandem! When transporting two single bicycles, I use a heavy blanket or mover's blanket between the two to protect them. When I want to transport my tandem, I use pipe insulation, available from hardware stores for just a few dollars, to protect the bikes' tubes, and I let the front end of the bike stick out of the back of the car. I use a bungee cord to close the hatchback over the bicycle, attaching one end to the closed latch of the hatchback door and the other end to the frame of the car.

WITH RACKS

Racks can be mounted to the rear or top of your vehicle.

Rear-mounted racks are relatively inexpensive and often quickly removable. Be careful not to mount the bike so that a tire is near the rear exhaust—you might find you've melted your tire.

Top-mounted models are more expensive and relatively permanent. They hold the bicycles well apart, preventing them from scraping against one another. Be careful about going into your garage with your bikes on top of your car!

BY AIRPLANE

PACKING OPTIONS
Bike Cases

Bike cases come in hard-shell and soft-shell models. Most have rollers and carrying straps. They cost up to several hundred dollars. Transporting your bicycle in a specially designed bicycle case may help protect your bicycle from damage. Airlines recognize bicycle cases as such and charge about $50 each way.

Cardboard Boxes

Boxes can usually be obtained free from airlines or bike stores. Stuff your clothes in plastic grocery store bags, pack them around your frame and wheels, and you'll rarely have any transportation damage. Pipe insulation or bubble wrap around your bike's tubes, for a couple of dollars, provides extra insurance against damage. Pad the ends of your hub axles to prevent them from poking through the sides of the box.

Airline Boxes. The ones from the airlines are oversized, poorly constructed, but convenient. When you are touring you don't want to concern yourself with storing bike cases or boxes. Many airlines will supply boxes only when you check in, so you'll need to plan ahead and arrive at the airport early.

If you are touring they can be useful because their large size often means that less disassembly is required. For example, using one may mean not having to remove fenders and racks. Some airlines will insure not only against loss but also against damage.

Manufacturer's Bike Boxes. Bike stores usually give these boxes away for free. They are sturdier and smaller than the airline variety.

Frame and Wheel Boxes. A bicycle can be broken down into two small boxes—a frame box and a wheel box. These boxes are small enough that you may not have to pay airline surcharges.

TOOLS REQUIRED FOR DISASSEMBLY AND ASSEMBLY

- Pedal wrench: thin 15-mm wrench or crescent
- Allen keys: 5- or 6-mm
- Crescent wrench if you have lock nuts on your wheels
- Perhaps a mallet or hammer
- Rag to wipe lube
- Lube for stem and seat post reassembly.

The disassembly of fenders and racks may require screwdrivers and small wrenches. It's possible to minimize the number of tools you'll need by having these accessories fastened with Allen bolts.

If using boxes, you'll also need the following:

- Packing insulation
- Tape
- Scissors

WHAT YOU'LL NEED TO DO TO PREPARE YOUR BIKE FOR A BIKE BOX

- Remove the pedals, not the cranks. The pedals screw back on easily, without any need for adjustment. It takes several rides for cranks to be properly retightened and for the right-hand crank's chain rings to be properly repositioned with respect to the front derailleur. Turning the axle of the left pedal clockwise loosens it. Turning the axle of the right pedal clockwise tightens it.

- Remove the handlebar and stem from frame.

  Use tape to mark the position of your stem. Remove the stem from the frame by loosening the stem bolt (D in the above diagram), normally located at the top of the stem in line with the head tube. Most often the bolt receives a 6-mm Allen wrench. The bolt has a wedge at the other end, holding the stem in place. It is usually necessary to hit the end of the bolt with a mallet, hammer, or perhaps the head

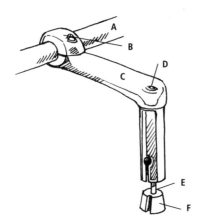

Parts of the stem
A—Handlebar
B—Handlebar-stem bolt
C—Stem body
D—Stem bolt, 6-mm Allen end
E—Stem bolt body
F—Wedge nut

of your crescent wrench to free the wedge. Pull the stem all the way out of the head tube. Be careful not to stretch or tear computer wires as you remove the handlebars.

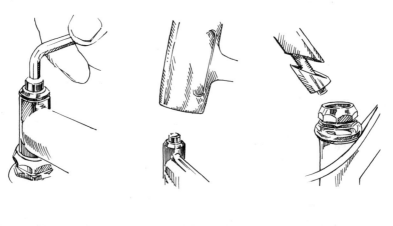

Loosen the stem.   Free the wedge.   Pull out the stem.

It may be necessary to release the front brake cable. Road bikers may also need to loosen the handlebar-stem bolt fixing the handlebar to the stem. Tape, bungee, or otherwise affix the bars along the top tube for packing.

• Remove seat and seat post. Use tape to mark the position of your seat post. Remove your seat and seat post from the frame by loosening the bolt holding the seat post to the frame. This usually requires a 5-mm Allen key. Mountain bikes often use a quick release here. Inexpensive bikes may use a hexbolt.

- Remove front wheel or both wheels. With most boxes, only the front wheel needs to be removed. Frame boxes require both wheels off. The sagging chain can be held up with a bungee cord wrapped around the frame, or it can be allowed to sag in the box.

- Perhaps remove rear derailleur. If you pack your bike in a bike box, shift your rear derailleur to the most inward position. This will help protect it from damage. If you are using a small box or case, it may be wise to remove the rear derailleur from the frame and tape it to the chain stay to protect it from damage.

- Perhaps remove brace dropouts. Packing skewers placed into dropouts help prevent damage and preserve the integrity of the frame and fork. Most bike stores have plenty of free plastic packing axles from the new bikes they receive. Better quality packing axles can also be easily made from old axles and nuts, or they can be purchased. Alternatively, remove the skewers from your wheels and tighten them loosely into the dropouts. Turning the forks around will allow the bike to fit in a smaller box.

- Perhaps remove fenders or racks. Fenders and racks must be removed for most cases and boxes.

- Gather small-objects bag. Place small objects such as quick-release skewers together in a larger bag. This will help prevent them from being lost through the cutout carrying holes or other holes in the box.

TRICKS

- Extra wheels can sometimes be taken on board, but usually not if they are recognized as such. Get an oversized garment bag. Usually you can put two wheels in one, and hang up your bag in the closet provided on most airplanes. Bubble-wrap envelopes large enough to enclose your wheels can be used to help protect them whether they are carried on or packed as luggage.

- Extra tape and scissors may help with last-minute fix-ups to your boxes. Take only small scissors in your carry-on luggage. Occasionally, airport security will confiscate large scissors.

- Pack your shoes and pedals with you in your carry-on bag. You can borrow a helmet or a bike if yours is lost, but shoes and matching cleated pedals are harder to find.

- Airplanes and cargo holds may have lower air pressure than is present on the ground. Let a little air out of your tires or they may burst. But leave some air in—it helps prevent damage to the tires, tubes, and rims.

- Frequent travelers: Have a prepackaged toiletries bag and first-aid kit that you use for trips. This will save you time and stress in repacking many small items.

- Be sure that all bags and boxes are labeled with your name, address, and telephone number. Place this information inside your luggage as well.

- Use curbside check-in if you can. If you have a buck or two in your hand, the skycap may take your container, rather than refer you to the airline check-in and a surcharge.

6

T R A I N I N G

GOALS

The best way to get somewhere is to know where you want to go. Set realistic and specific goals. Keep the long view, but also establish intermediate goals. Analyze your strengths and weaknesses. Figure out what aspects of fitness or training you'll need. Monitor and chart your progress. Reward yourself as you reach your milestones.

As an example, let's suppose that after a couple of years of riding, your goal is to ride 100 miles in one day—a century event. What training tips might you keep in mind?

TRAINING PRINCIPLES

Here are guidelines to keep in mind when following any training program.

Follow your own program: Some riders are faster and stronger, some are slower and weaker. Some are relatively new to riding and some have been riding for years. Get hints and advice from others, but remember your training program is not the same as every one else's.

Build up: You are at a certain place now and you may know where you want to be. Get there gradually, building up your miles and speed to reach your goals. Don't expect to get there in one big step.

Challenge yourself: We get stronger by challenging the body. As our body adapts to training, we can continue to improve by taking on new challenges.

Be organized: Have a program. Organize your schedule to allow you to stick to your program. Think ahead. Keep lists. It's tough to ride home from the office if you've forgotten your bicycling shoes. It's tough to ride Wednesday evening if you've forgotten to clear the decks and you have to take your child to softball practice.

Do the same workouts, do different workouts: By repeating the same or similar workouts, you'll learn how hard you can go and how and when to work harder. But changing your workouts every month or so keeps you mentally fresh and trains different aspects of fitness.

Be flexible: It rains. You get sick. Adversity strikes. Don't brood or become upset about it. Modify your program, if needed, and get on with your training.

Track your progress: Keep a record or log of how you're doing. Review it every week or two. It will let you know if you are on track and whether your program is working or needs adjustments.

Keep it fun: Don't be a slave to your training. Keep your overall goals in mind, but don't become obsessed about the details. If your schedule calls for intervals (hard, intermittent efforts) but you're sick of them, do something else.

Rest: It's easy to get caught up in any program. Your program is important, but keep it in perspective and make sure that you allow proper time to recover and for other noncycling activities. Avoid overtraining. Give yourself at least a day or two off each week.

Reward yourself: Riding and finishing an event are often a big reward in themselves. Consider other rewards along the way. Completed the first six weeks of your training on track? Reward yourself with a new pair of cycling shoes. Or a dinner on the town to thank someone for putting up with you!

WORKOUTS

The two big variables are volume and intensity. Consider how these variables might apply in training to ride a century:

VOLUME—HOW MUCH

Volume can be measured in terms of distance or time.

You are going to ride 100 miles. So you've got to train to be able to ride that far. That means going on rides that are progressively longer and longer, building up to be able to cover the distance. You have to ride 100 miles only once. You don't have to ride that far repeatedly in training, but you do have to be able to ride a minimum of 70 miles by the end of your training program.

INTENSITY—HOW HARD

Think about three levels of intensity: The intensity level you will ride at in the century is your average pace. You can train at that level, below that level, or above that level.

Below pace are rides at a level below your average century pace. These are for active recovery riding or relative rest days. Normally your heart rate at below race pace will be under 65 to 70 percent of your maximum.

Pace or endurance training is riding at the level of intensity you hope to sustain during the century. Normally this will be at a heart rate 70 to 85 percent of your maximum.

Above pace is riding faster than the average pace you will ride during the century. This type of training includes interval training. Normally this will be at a heart rate above 80 to 85 percent of your maximum.

KEEPING A TRAINING DIARY

Recording your workouts is a popular and helpful way to improve your training. By keeping track of the volume and intensity of your workouts, you'll gain insight into how your body responds to training, keep track of your schedule, and improve your motivation, too.

You'll want to record the distance or time you rode and the difficulty of your workout. Most riders make a notation of where and with whom they rode. Some riders record how many feet they ascended. This is easy with an altitude bicycle computer. Many riders also like to keep track of their morning weight and rest pulse. I record my training on a simple form, one month to a sheet of paper. A sample training log is included in appendix B.

TRAINING

Sometimes you'll find yourself training with riders who are stronger or weaker than you are. If they are stronger, you may have to work very hard to keep up, especially if they don't accommodate you. But what if they are not as strong as you? Can you still get a good workout? Yes!

I often go on training rides (or even tours) with my wife, who is a good rider but not as strong as I am. I have developed lots of fun things to do so that we both get a good workout.

On the hills, I push her. I hold one hand on the handlebar, close to the stem for control, and I place the other hand on the flat of her back and push. She works as hard as she can and so do I.

Alternatively, I can go up the hills with only one leg. I unclip from my right pedal, and, in an easy gear, pedal with my left leg for a minute or two. Then I clip back in, spin a little, and do the one-leg work with my right leg. I get an excellent power workout, and it sure slows me down.

Or I can decide that I'm only going to use one gear for the whole ride—for example, a 39/15. That means that on the steep sections I work really hard and go slowly. On the downhills I have to spin like crazy or coast.

You can come up with more ideas yourself. There are many ways you can ride with others, regardless of a difference in riding speed and strength, and still get a good workout—and they can enjoy the training, too.

HILLS

Hills present a special challenge. When you ride on the level, you can ease up and rest and still make forward progress. But hills are different. You have to keep putting out a pretty good level of energy just to avoid falling over.

It really pays to psych yourself to like the hills—they will be hard at first, but they are really one of the best ways to get stronger and become more confident on your bike. Hills are great concentrated workouts.

Of course, climbing hills is only half of the equation. On the other side, there's descending. For some riders, descending, especially hills with corners, is scary. Fortunately, descending skills and techniques can be learned so that what was an intimidating descent can become great fun.

GETTING UP

Here are my favorite hints for getting up hills.

Get the Right Gears, Shift Early

Many riders don't have "easy" enough gears to allow them to climb comfortably. There is no shame in having easy gears. The first few races I entered I had a 26-cog on my rear wheel. My competition had 21s. They did make comments about my "easy gears." But when I won every one of my first few races, they didn't laugh at me anymore—they asked where they could buy a similar setup.

There is no shame in having a triple chain ring setup on a road bike. (Mountain bikes come with a third chain ring.) Some bike stores will tell you that it won't work to change your standard road setup, but triples do work. Find a mechanic to help you change your gearing if you need the gears.

I set up my wife, Gero, with a triple chain ring (taken from our mountain bike) for a hard mountain ride she was doing, and she liked it so much she's kept it on ever since. She doesn't need the small ring very often, but she says that when she does, when others are standing, puffing, and panting, she just slips into the small chain ring and rides past them.

New riders frequently use their muscles until they can't push any more. When their legs bog down, they shift to an easier gear—if they have one. But by then it may be too late. The muscles may be exhausted and unable to continue, even in a "bail-out," or super-easy, gear.

It's a much better strategy to shift early to easier gears. Save your legs. If you find that you are going well, you can always shift to a harder gear later. This is the strategy used by most top professional racers. On a hard, steady climb, top pros shift to harder gears, not easier ones, halfway up the hill.

Mash or Spin?

Many fit riders find they get up the hill fastest when they mash—riding a hard gear at a slow cadence. Until you're strong enough to confidently reach the top working hard all the way, spin from time to time—ride in an easy gear, maintaining a fluid stroke, pulling up as well as pushing down.

Be Conservative, Go Easy

If hills intimidate you, or are your weak link, take it easy. Go 5 to 10 percent easier than you think you need to. Conserve. You can always pick it up later. If you are a great hill climber, the opposite strategy may hold. You obtain an overall better time by working a little harder on the hills.

TRAIN ON THE HILLS

It's obvious, of course, but riding the hills makes you better on the hills. It's astonishing how many riders are disappointed by their slow progress on hills—and when I ask them whether they train on hills, often their answer is no.

Steady hill riding, interval hill riding, big-gear hill riding, hill sprints: Incorporate them into your program and you'll certainly climb better.

Get the Proper Position

Sure, bent over in the drops is the efficient way to fly along on level ground. But hills are different. Aerodynamic resistance is much less of a concern, because speeds are lower.

You get the most power sitting up as high as you can. So place your hands on the tops of the handlebars—that's where they belong. Most riders do better by pushing back on the saddle and pushing forward with the legs, rather than down.

Sit or Stand?

Everyone has an individual preference. Most of us do better sitting on long climbs, but everyone needs a change in position from time to time, and standing helps work different muscle groups and gives a partial rest to some leg and back muscles.

A minority of riders, especially light riders, climb better standing.

Establish a Breathing Rhythm

"Getting a rhythm"—it's something you'll hear when Phil Ligett comments on the top pro riders in the big races. Concentrate on each stroke. Coordinate your breathing with your legs. Perhaps take a breath every one and a half revolutions of your legs. You'll go faster!

Relax

Don't get tied up in knots on the climb. Relax your arms, relax your shoulders. Relax your back. Use your legs.

GETTING DOWN

For years I've coached a group of Masters women. We meet regularly at Metropolitan Boulevard in central San Diego county. Our ride is a 0.75-mile loop. It is 0.3-mile uphill, 0.3-mile downhill, with two very short, almost nonexistent flat sections in between. The workout has become one of intervals—relatively short, hard efforts.

Although those uphill intervals are killers, even more difficult for many of the women is the quick descent, which leads into a right-hand turn. At first, most of the women brake all the way down the hill. Later, as they become more skilled, they are able to coast down the hill without breaking and make the corner.

Finally, after twenty or thirty sessions, each session with about a dozen laps, they are able to attack the descent and take the corner at full speed, often at more than 30 miles per hour.

Here's what I teach them:

• Learn the proper techniques and always feel in control.

Don't scare yourself. Some people think you have to "get your feet wet" by going down big hills. Not at all! Practice on gentle descents and gentle corners first. As you improve, you'll be able to tackle those bigger hills.

• Concentrate on where you are going. Look around the corner to where you will be.

A common error is looking down at the road just in front of you. Don't look at the corner just ahead or at the road beneath you. The great hockey player Wayne Gretzky said, "I don't skate to where the puck is, I skate to where it will be." If you look farther down the road, your body and bike will follow your mind, and you'll ride faster, more safely, and more comfortably down the hill.

• Brake before you reach corners, not while in corners.

If you brake while in the corner, you'll have less control of the bicycle and be losing momentum as you exit the corner. If you brake before the corner, you'll have much greater control while cornering and be able to accelerate as you leave the corner. This will result in overall faster speed.

- Put your outside leg down.

    Straighten out your outside leg. Put weight on your outside leg. This technique increases your stability while cornering and lifts your inside foot away from the ground when you lean.

- Put weight on your inside hand.

    This is an important advanced technique for cornering. As the bike balances between your outside leg and inside hand, lean the bike more than your body. You'll be better able to control the bicycle and respond to changes in the radius of the turn.

HEART-RATE MONITORING

Heart-rate monitors allow you to observe your heart rate while working out. This has revolutionized modern approaches to training. They are also fun and interesting. Although you can feel your pulse to count your heart rate, that isn't practical or accurate at high work intensities.

WHY USE A HEART-RATE MONITOR?

- Monitors are used in designing and implementing training and racing programs.

    A heart-rate monitor allows you to ensure that you work according to plan. A monitor helps make sure that you work hard enough. It also helps make sure that you don't work too hard.

- Monitors help analyze how you feel and what happens in training and in races. For some riders, monitors don't necessarily change their training, but permit an understanding of what is going on.

- Monitors improve motivation. The feedback they provide is engaging for many riders.

MAXIMUM HEART RATE

Maximum heart rate is the highest heart rate you can achieve. Determining maximum heart rate is the first step in developing a heart-rate training program. For most riders, heart-rate zones for aerobic, threshold, and anaerobic work are determined from maximum HR. Many coaches and athletes attempt to determine max HR a few times a year to set training intensities.

Individualize Your Numbers

It's a popular misconception that your maximum heart rate equals 220 minus your age. This rule-of-thumb is usually not helpful. The statistical average for the population is useless for the individual. It's like saying the average person is 5'9" tall, so all bikes should be made 55 cm.

Determination of Max Heart Rate with a Heart-Rate Monitor

To obtain a max HR value, you need to be:

1. Rested

2. Well warmed up

3. Motivated to make a maximum effort

Why rested? Rest provides for recovery from previous exertion. With muscle fatigue, soreness, or a lack of glycogen, it is not possible to produce a maximal effort.

Why a warm-up? Max HR depends upon maximum cardiovascular demand. If you are not well warmed up, there's less blood flowing to your working muscles (the precapillary sphincters are not all open)—maximum effort cannot elicit maximum response.

Why motivated? Many people see their max only in a race or a test in which they are really motivated. It's often difficult for riders to test their max when by themselves.

There are any number of different ways to find your max HR. Here is one way:

Warm up for at least 5 to 10 minutes. After working at a moderate pace for 3 minutes, increase your effort by about 10 percent every minute. This means either increasing your cadence by 5 to 10 revolutions per minute, or increasing your gearing by one gear of difficulty every couple of minutes.

When you get to the point where it is extremely difficult to continue at pace, sprint absolutely as hard as you can for 30 seconds. Watch your heart monitor. This value should be close to your maximum.

TRAINING

109

RESTING HEART RATE

Resting heart rate provides a tool for monitoring fitness and recovery from training. It is determined by counting or monitoring your heart rate while not engaged in physical activity. This is usually measured first thing in the morning while lying still in bed. Conventional wisdom states that resting heart rate is a measure of fitness and recovery. As you get fitter, your resting heart rate falls. When you are not recovered, your resting heart rate rises.

Use resting heart rate as a tool in evaluation, but don't get spooked by high values: Some riders have their best performances on days when their resting heart rates are high.

My own resting heart rate is a lot higher than that of many of my friends and certainly higher than that of most racers—it's about 60. That's just normal for me, so I don't get concerned.

Factors Affecting Resting HR

Dehydration, fever or other illness, drugs, stress, or the environment might raise resting heart rate. For many riders, the discomfort of a full bladder, the physical activity of getting up to urinate, or the jarring of an alarm clock will raise heart rate. Resting quietly in bed for several minutes after returning from urinating or after turning the alarm clock off will give a more accurate reading. The value measured while lying flat on the back is often slightly lower than that measured while lying on the side.

THRESHOLD HEART RATE

The heart rate that you can sustain for prolonged efforts is important in prescribing exercise training and as a measure of fitness. For example, elite athletes can sustain 92 percent of their maximum heart rates for events lasting about an hour. For events longer than this, the percentage will be lower. For shorter events, the percentage will be higher. Beginners who have gained strength and endurance can ride at about 80 percent of their maximum heart rate.

FACTORS AFFECTING HEART RATE

A variety of individual and environmental factors affect heart rate.

Interpreting heart rate in the context of these factors provides better insight into the meaning of heart rates.

Temperature

Heart rates may be one beat higher for every 2 or 3 degrees above 70°F. Cold weather results in lower heart rates.

Altitude

At altitude, threshold and max HR are reduced about one beat for every 1,000 feet of elevation for athletes who have trained at sea level.

Dehydration

Dehydration places increased demands upon the cardiovascular system. For a given power output, heart rates are increased.

Fitness

As most athletes become fitter, they improve their cardiovascular function and increase their sport-specific muscle mass—they are able to achieve higher maximal heart rates.

As athletes become fitter, they are able to produce more power for a given heart rate, or produce the same power with a lower heart rate.

Medications/Drugs

Drugs may decrease or increase heart rate. For example, beta-blockers, commonly used to treat high blood pressure and migraines, lower heart rate. Decongestants, asthma medicines, and caffeine raise heart rates.

Illness or Disease

Medical conditions can decrease or increase heart rate. For example, an overactive thyroid can raise heart rate, and an underactive one lower it.

HEART-RATE TRAINING ZONES

You can establish heart-rate training zones based on percentages of your maximum heart rate. There are many "zone" systems. The following is a simple system to understand.

Heart-Rate Ranges/Zones

	% Max HR	Effort
Noodling	<65%	Recovery, easy—"Below pace"
Aerobic	66–85%	Group rides, warm-ups—"Pace"
Threshold	80–92%	Time trials—"Above pace"
Anaerobic	>93%	Jumps, intervals, sprints

Noodling

Riding under 65 percent of your maximum heart rate is easy riding. If your maximum is about 180 beats per minute, your noodling rate is under 120 beats per minute. This is recovery riding.

Aerobic Training

Working between 66 and 85 percent of your max HR is training aerobically—"with oxygen."

Heart-rate economy will improve: As you become fitter, you will be able to accomplish the same work at lower heart rates. Put another way, you will be able to accomplish more work at the same heart rate. Recovery heart rate will improve: The fitter you are, the faster your heart rate will recover from hard efforts.

Threshold Training

This is working between 80 and 92 percent of your max heart rate. You are at the border between aerobic and anaerobic work. This level of work is sustainable for up to an hour. Training at this level some of the time will improve your fitness.

Your threshold level will rise: New riders can commonly sustain 80 percent of maximum heart rate for an hour. As fitness improves, levels closer to 92 percent of max heart rate can be maintained.

Anaerobic Training and Racing

Heart rates of 93 percent or more of your max HR can't be kept up for very long. This is very hard work. You get these efforts in jumps, intervals, and sprints: red-line stuff. Not what most commuters, weekend riders, or century riders need.

Training Time Needed to Progress

To train the aerobic system, riders ideally need high-aerobic work—80 to 85 percent of maximum heart rate—for at least 30 minutes, three times a week.

HEART-RATE TRAINING ISN'T EVERYTHING

Although heart-rate monitoring has revolutionized training, it's not a be-all and end-all. While heart rate is one measure of training intensity, it's not always the appropriate way to measure intensity. Not everyone finds that heart-rate monitoring improves performance. And not everyone can figure out the buttons or can process the data on a heart-rate monitor.

Heart Training is Specific

When you are training, you must consider your purpose. Are you training to get the maximum heart workout? Are you training to get the maximum leg strength? Are you training to ride the fastest you can, right now?

Strength Training

You'll end up stronger by having "separate" workouts or aspects of workouts for leg strength and power. The legs develop more strength in bigger gears. But when you ride big gears, the intensity of your workout is not matched by your heart rate.

For example, it is not unusual for riders to train in big gears going up hills at 75 percent of maximum heart rate. Exertion may be similar to that perceived while riding at 85 percent of max heart rate in a smaller gear.

Unreliable for Anaerobic Work

Although heart-rate readings of 93 percent or more of your max are anaerobic, not all anaerobic efforts will result in heart rates in this range. Your heart responds to changing exercise intensity, but this response lags behind true effort. And monitor readings lag behind true heart rate by several seconds. These lags mean that you may already be recovering before your monitor has had the time to reflect true effort.

Don't Be a Slave to Your Monitor

Riding under 65 percent of your max HR? You are not training your heart but that may not be necessary. Recently I started training with new aerobars. I wanted to get used to the position. I was not training for leg strength. I was not training for leg speed. I was training for position and comfort.

I rode an easy workout at a heart rate of 110 beats per minute. I was training. I was training my back muscles and my forearms. I was resting my legs, and recovering from a hard Sunday ride. Recovering—that is an important part of training, too!

7

DIET AND NUTRITION

Y ou know the saying, "You are what you eat." The question is, What do you eat? And drink? What do you need to put in your body so that your legs keep going round and your heart keeps beating?

NUTRITION BASICS

I've always been fascinated by nutrition and the role it might play in living a long and healthy life. I still remember reading, being influenced by, and saving, an article written by Alexander Leaf twenty-five years ago in *Scientific American*. It was called "Getting Old." Dr. Leaf visited and reported on longevity in Hunza, Pakistan, in Vilcabamba, Ecuador, and in the highlands of Georgia, in the Soviet Caucasus.

Although some of his original reporting and research has since been challenged, it remains a fascinating article. Every month almost every woman's magazine has another diet or nutritional theory, but although many fads and theories have come and gone, I'm still drawn to my old conclusions:

- Eat a variety of whole, unprocessed foods.
- Control your weight.

- Eat a diet relatively high in fiber.
- Eat a diet relatively low in high-cholesterol foods and fat.
- Eat lots of fruits and vegetables.
- Eat regular meals.
- Eat fewer simple sugars—candy, table sugar, "sweets."
- Avoid junk food.
- Avoid salty foods.
- Drink little, if any, alcohol.
- Make dietary changes gradually.
- Learn about your body, and whether high blood pressure, diabetes, blood cholesterol, or other factors should influence your diet.
- Rely on food, not pills, for your nutrients, though consider an inexpensive multivitamin-multimineral supplement.
- Don't worry about occasional dietary indiscretions (as long as they are only occasional).

GENERAL PRINCIPLES OF NUTRITION

The best current thinking is still what my parents told me: You can get everything you need from what you eat. Rely on a variety of whole, unprocessed foods. Have food items in balance, and in moderation.

No one food supplies all of the many vitamins and minerals that we need. And there are probably still nutrients yet to be discovered. Relying on a variety of foods, rather than pills or chemicals, means that these as-yet unknown substances may still be part of our diets.

Too much or too little of many foods is harmful. It's like tire pressure. Too little air and you have too much rolling resistance. Too much and the bike handles skittishly. And both too much and too little risk flat tires—whether pinch flats or blowouts.

There are no truly "good" or "bad" foods. It's all a question of moderation. The USDA nutrition pyramid is an excellent guideline. Make carbohydrates (pasta, potatoes, rice, breads, and cereals) the center of your meals. Eat lots of fruits and vegetables. Add relatively small quantities of protein and fat for their nutritional balance, taste, and variety. It's not magical or difficult.

Food Guide Pyramid.

The recommended "healthful diet" for the general population is very close to the same diet that is recommended for specialized high-endurance aerobic athletes such as century riders: high in carbohydrates, low in fats, and low in cholesterol. The minor variations are discussed below.

Although active athletes may require more nutrients than the general population, the increased calories they consume usually compensate for their increased requirements.

VITAMINS AND MINERALS

Many of us do not eat properly. Women need to be concerned about getting enough iron and calcium. Zinc deficiency is a potential problem in all athletes.

It is reasonable to take a single multiple-vitamin multimineral tablet daily to help ensure you get everything you need. In general, taking many tablets of different formulations is probably a waste of money.

EXTRA SODIUM?

It is true that long rides, day after day, especially in the heat, can deplete your body's sodium. Since most of us ride only a few hours at a time, sodium is not usually a problem. But if you train several days in a row or ride ultra cycling events, consider adding salt to your diet.

CARBOHYDRATES—FUEL FOR ENDURANCE AEROBIC ATHLETES

Aerobic athletic performance demands glycogen, a storage form of carbohydrate. Your body makes glycogen from the carbohydrates you ingest, not from fat or protein.

Your body can store about 2,000 calories in glycogen. If you exercise for more than an average of an hour daily, there's a good chance that a diet high in carbohydrates and low in fat will help your body make glycogen and continue to perform at a high level.

CARBO LOADING

It's a technique you've probably heard about—increasing your intake of complex carbohydrates for a few days before a long aerobic endurance event can boost performance. It's probably helpful, so scoop up the pasta, potatoes, and breads before that long ride or century.

PRERIDE NUTRITION

Your mother was right, a good breakfast is central to a good start on the day. It never ceases to amaze me how some riders take off without a good breakfast.

If you are performing an all-out mile race at 7:00 A.M., perhaps a big breakfast isn't a good idea. But if you are expecting to go out and ride for a few hours, fuel your body.

A half-hour before you ride, you want to pump your energy supplies and make sure that you are well hydrated. Here again, a high-carbohydrate, low-fat diet works best for most riders.

WITHIN-THE-RIDE NUTRITION

Riding for more than an hour? Continue to fuel your body with high-carbohydrate, low-fat foods. You'll be able to go farther and faster if you do.

SPORTS DRINKS

From the original Gatorade to the modern metabolic optimizers, these beverages mostly help you hydrate and get a few calories. They can be more expensive than one-half to one-third strength fruit juice, which is my preferred beverage while riding. But for those who have difficulty tolerating fruit sugar, they can be very useful.

ENERGY BARS

They're convenient sources of calories while you're riding, and they fit in your jersey pocket. They may also have additives like guarana (caffeine) and ma huang (ephedra, an adrenalinelike chemical), which you may or may not want to be eating.

Most of them add vitamins and minerals to help justify their cost— because per calorie they are expensive. Fat-free fig bars, bananas, or homemade low-fat cookies are often a good, cheap alternative.

CARBOHYDRATE GELS

It's not a solid, it's not a drink. It's a gel that you squirt in your mouth and then chase with 8 ounces or more of fluid. It's another convenient, relatively expensive source of calories for the active athlete.

POST-RIDE NUTRITION

Even if you've had a good breakfast, even if you've fueled while riding, after your long ride you're still almost certainly calorically depleted. Replenishing your body's carbohydrates with a few hundred calories within the first half hour after a ride, and then again within the next two hours, will do a lot to help you recover, replace your glycogen, and ride again the next day if you like.

HYDRATION

Yes, it is water that you chiefly need when riding. And yes, you should drink before you are thirsty. Clear, nonconcentrated urine is an indication of appropriate rehydration. Dark urine can be a warning that you are dehydrated and need to drink a lot.

A dilute carbohydrate solution (about 5 percent sugar) is almost always a better choice than plain water. It tastes better, encourages you to drink, and helps replace some lost calories.

TRYING OUT NEW FOODS

Experiment on your training rides, and find out what suits you best.

Don't try out new food or drink on "the big day." For more detailed information and theory about nutrition, read *Bicycling Medicine* (see appendix A, For More Information).

8

HOW TO FIX
A FLAT TIRE

Many bicycles sit unused in American garages because owners are daunted by the task of either fixing the flat or taking the bike to a bike store for repair.

It is true that beginners can spend up to 1 hour trying to fix a flat. And it is true that sometimes they are not successful, even after all that effort. But by following these instructions, most people should be able to fix a flat in under 10 minutes. Experts can fix one in under 3 minutes.

Here are the steps to fixing a flat:

1. Remove the wheel from the bicycle frame.

2. Remove one side of the tire from the wheel.

3. Remove the tube.

4. Find the leak.

5. If possible, determine the cause of the flat.

6. Check whether the tire needs replacing.

7. Replace or patch the tube.

8. Replace the tube under the tire, on the rim.

9. Replace the tire on the wheel.

10. Replace the wheel on the bicycle frame.

SAFETY FIRST

If you've flatted while riding, find a safe place to fix your flat. Don't stop where traffic makes repairs unsafe.

EQUIPMENT NEEDED

- Wrench to remove wheel from frame if you don't have a quick release
- Tire irons
- Patch kit or spare tube
- Pump

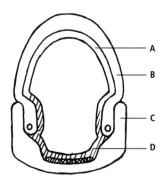

Wheel Cross Section
A—Tube
B—Tire
C—Rim
D—Rim strip

STEP 1. REMOVE WHEEL FROM BICYCLE FRAME

If you've flatted the rear wheel, shift your rear derailleur to the smallest cog—that's the hardest gear, the one on the outside near the frame. This will make removing the rear wheel easier.

If you're using wide tires, you may need to loosen the brake cable to allow the tire to pass through the brake pads. Normally there is a quick-release mechanism near the brake or near the brake lever that allows you to do this in a second.

Some bicycles have tabs on the forks to prevent the front wheel from coming off accidentally. If this is the case, you may need not only to release the quick release but also to unscrew the bolt.

If you are using fastened bolts, you'll need a wrench to loosen them. Bolts loosen counterclockwise and tighten clockwise.

STEP 2. REMOVE ONE SIDE OF THE TIRE FROM WHEEL

If air remains in the tube, deflate the tube completely.

Use plastic tire irons designed for this job, not screwdrivers or other objects, which frequently result in more tube punctures.

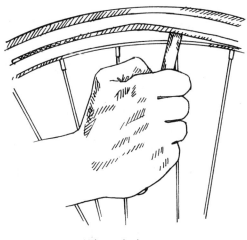

Using a tire iron.

Insert the tire iron under one side or bead of the tire away from the valve, pry the side of the tire off the rim, and slide the tire iron along the rim to roll off the rest of the bead of the tire. Leave the inner bead of the tire sitting on the rim. If after placing the first tire iron you are unable to slide it, use two tire irons to work the tire edge off.

(It is possible to remove a tire without tire irons, though it is difficult. In order to perform this trick, free the contact between the tire edge and rim lip, compress the tire into the center hollow of the rim, and force the tire on the other side of the rim over the rim.)

STEP 3. REMOVE THE TUBE

There may be a knurled nut on the tube's valve stem that must be unscrewed to release the tube. Pull out the tube, finishing at the valve.

Once it's out, keep the orientation of the tube constant with the wheel. This will help you identify the cause after you've found the leak.

STEP 4. FIND THE HOLE

Pump up the tube. You will probably hear the hole before you see it. Pass every inch of the tube by your ear to detect the leak. If that doesn't work, pass the tube by your mouth and you may feel the escaping air on your upper lip. With minuscule leaks, you may need to insert the tube in water and watch for a trail of bubbles.

STEP 5. FIND THE CAUSE OF THE FLAT

It's important to try to determine the cause of the flat. If you don't, and the cause remains, there's a good chance that you'll flat immediately again.

Inflate the flatted tube and hold it up to the wheel to determine the position of the problem. The leak may correspond to a foreign object stuck in the tire or to slippage or a tear of the rim strip. It's not always possible to find the cause, but here's what to check for:

PUNCTURES

These are the most common cause of flats. Check the tire for thorns or bits of glass, especially at the point where the hole in the tube was found. Remove the culprit carefully.

Sometimes, just by casually inspecting the tire you may see a piece of glass or thorn sticking out of the tire. Usually you need to feel the inner surface of the tire carefully. Occasionally you need to match the tire to the hole in the tube to find the tiny villain.

SNAKEBITES

Snakebite flats are usually caused by the tire and tube being pinched between the road and the rim, causing two small holes in the tube that look like a snakebite.

The usual causes are underinflation, too narrow a tire for your weight, or hitting something (such as a rock or pothole) while having your full weight on the tire. The solutions are to make sure your tires are inflated properly, use a larger-size tire if you weigh a lot, and either avoid rocks and potholes or stand up with your knees and elbows flexed (to act as shock absorbers) when you go over them.

PINCHED TUBES

This happened because a bit of your inner tube was pinched between your tire bead and your rim. It is usually caused by an error in mounting the tube and tire, although occasionally a tire defect or a mismatch between rim size and tire size is to blame.

LESS COMMON CAUSES

Inadequate Rim Strip

Spoked rims have holes for the spoke nipples. These are covered with a rim strip that prevents the tube from pushing through the hole and bursting. But sometimes the rim strip creeps, or moves, uncovering the spoke holes, and sometimes the rim strip breaks down.

Protruding Spokes

Improperly assembled wheels occasionally have spoke ends that protrude through the rim strip and puncture the tube.

Valve Failure

Occasionally the seals or other mechanical components of the tube's valve will wear out or break, making it impossible for the tube to hold air.

Tube Failure

It's possible that a manufacturing defect causes a flat tire, but this cause is listed last because it is the rarest. Defects around the valve-tube junction are the most common type of manufacturing tube failures.

STEP 6. CHECK THE TIRE

Of course you've run your finger along the inside of the tire to check for a thorn, bit of glass, or other cause of a puncture. But you must do more because not only may the tube have been punctured, but also the tire. It's possible that a new tube will not be contained by the tire and will quickly explode. Riding too long on a flat tire before stopping may destroy a tire.

Small defects require no treatment. Moderate defects can be temporarily covered and supported or booted with a tube patch, dollar bill, or other material. Large defects are unsafe for riding.

Occasionally a tire is simply worn, old, or has suffered a defect and should be replaced. If your tire has its threads showing, if the sidewalls have been punctured, or if the tire is checkered and brittle from wear or exposure to ultraviolet light, it's time to replace it.

STEP 7. REPLACE OR PATCH THE TUBE

Most riders out on day rides, especially on group rides, are best served by having a spare tube and simply replacing the tube. This takes less time than patching a tube. The tube can be patched after the ride is over. Do carry a patch kit, though, in case of a second flat.

To patch a tube, you'll need a patch kit. A patch kit contains patches, a small tube of glue, and a small square of sandpaper. First, roughen the surface around the hole of a dry tube with the sandpaper. Then apply glue over an area larger than the patch you will use and allow it to dry for about a minute. Finally, without touching the contact surface of the patch, apply it to the tube.

Some modern patches do not require glue. They cost a little more, but they are very easy to apply and convenient. They may not form as permanent a seal as traditional glue-on patches.

After patching, reinflate the tube to check for other holes.

STEP 8. REPLACE TUBE UNDER TIRE, ON RIM

Inflate the tube just enough for it to hold its shape. Too much inflation and it won't fit inside the tire. Too little (or none) and you are likely to pinch it while installing the tire.

If using a new Presta tube, remove the knurled nut from the valve stem. Insert the valve stem.

Fit the tube inside the tire, all the way around.

STEP 9. REPLACE TIRE ON RIM

Reattach the tire to the rim, starting about 90 degrees away from the valve stem. Work the tire onto the rim moving first toward the valve stem. Finish away from the valve stem.

Just before you are finished installing the tire, deflate the tube. Use both thumbs and middle and ring fingers to roll and push the last part of the tire over the rim. Tires are often a tight fit, so this can be the most

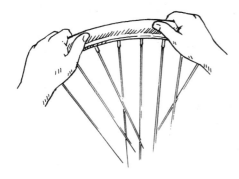

Replacing the tire: Press with both thumbs, rolling toward your middle and ring fingers.

difficult part and take some practice. Try to avoid using tire irons, since it's easy to puncture a tube with them.

Press the valve stem through the rim back up into the tire and allow it to return downward. This helps correctly seat the thicker valve stem area within the tire, preventing it from being pinched. Inflate the tire to about 20 psi and move the tire back and forth, making sure no part of the inner tube is pinched.

If you are on the road or trail, you'll estimate how much air to pump in by experience or feel—or you'll stop when you're tired of pumping and pressure seems "enough." When using a floor pump, inflate the tire to its rated pressure.

STEP 10. REPLACE WHEEL ON BICYCLE FRAME

To replace the rear wheel, pull the derailleur backward, set the smallest cog on the chain, release the derailleur and pop the axle in the dropouts.

Although it is possible to insert wheels in dropouts while bikes are on repair stands or lying flat on the ground, wheels seat and center properly in the frame only when installed while the bike is upright, resting on its wheels.

Tighten the brake cable if you've previously loosened it. Check that the wheel is centered on the frame between the chainstays and between the brake pads.

SPECIAL NOTES AND TRICKS

Presta valves are skinnier, the Schraeders are thicker. Schraeder valves are slightly more difficult to inflate than Prestas. Presta are the standard of the bike industry, but Schraeder valves are the standard of the car industry, and that's what garages have.

If you fix a flat and you flat again and again, it's pretty frustrating. Sometimes you must replace the tube and tire to break this cycle, because of a thorn or piece of glass you just can't find. Some riders and some manufacturers apply talc to their tubes before installing them to create a slippery surface that resists pinching and flats.

Keep the tire label positioned consistently with respect to the valve stem. This way you will be easily able to orient tube defects to a specific tire location. Hold a hand pump steady, with your thumb positioned over the tire. It is possible to break a valve stem by forcefully bending it while pumping. Steadying the wheel against a solid object, such as a wall, makes inflating the tire easier.

To prevent flats, keep your tires properly inflated. Check your tires before every ride and replace worn tires. Use tires matched to your rims and to your body weight. While riding, watch for and avoid glass or sharp objects, especially in the "unused triangles" present at all intersections. Learn to unweight the bike when riding over bumps, curbs, and holes, and, finally, check your rim strips every six months or whenever you have a flat.

9

COMMON QUESTIONS

DO I NEED TO STRETCH?

A stretching program is part of any overall fitness plan and it can help you recover from rides and prevent or treat muscle soreness. Stretching the hamstrings allows you to ride with a higher saddle position, which improves your cycling power and performance. It doesn't take long to stretch. You can perform a good routine in just 10 minutes, or you can spend a lot longer if you have the time. Stretching exercises are available from many sources, including Bob Anderson's book *Stretching*, which is listed in the appendix.

HOW SHOULD I TREAT ROAD RASH?

Road rash is the bicyclist's term for scraped skin. Falling is an occasional occupational hazard for the rider just learning how to balance or the racer.

Everyone knows the importance of cleaning a wound as soon as possible. The real trick is in keeping the scraped skin covered for at least a week to prevent scab formation. At least once a day take a warm bath or shower. Keep the area moist with antibiotic cream and cover with Vaseline gauze or other preparations. After a few days a whitish, soft scab will begin to form. Gently rub this off with a washcloth. The prevention of scab formation means that oxygen from the air can more easily reach the newly forming skin, and healing is then measurably faster.

WHAT ABOUT KNEE INJURIES?

Overuse knee injuries are occasionally a problem. A combination of improper bicycle position or too much too soon is often responsible.

In general, pain in the front of the knee is helped by a higher saddle position, pain in the back of the knee by a lower position and hamstring stretches. Pain at the outside or inside edges often is related to fixed (non-floating, or nonrotating) cleats. Repositioning the cleat to allow your toe to point more toward the side of the knee that hurts often helps.

HOW DO I RECOVER?

After a long, hard ride, drink and eat to replace lost fluids and calories. Have a warm shower and stretch. Horizontal activity—a nap, relaxing with TV, a movie, or a book—also helps.

It's easy to get burnt out, especially if you are enthusiastic and try to do too much too soon. Be sure to take off some days every week at the beginning of your training. Even elite athletes commonly take off a day or two every week. Rest is important!

DOES MASSAGE HELP?

Many riders and racers find that massage seems to help their recovery. And many cyclists certainly enjoy a good rub.

Is there scientific proof that massage improves cycling? No, not exactly. But so many racers report feeling so much better after a massage that it's probably a good idea for them.

WOMEN ASK: HOW DO I FIND
A COMFORTABLE SADDLE?

Perhaps the biggest problem women have is finding a comfortable saddle. It's also an occasional problem for men. Whereas men all have basically the same shape pelvis, women have one of four shapes, so no one saddle fits all women.

Finding a comfortable saddle is often a matter of trial and error.

For the sake of enjoying your riding, it's worth experimenting to find a saddle that works for you. Some saddles specially designed for women tend to work well. Terry, a company that manufactures many products for women, markets saddles that work well for many of my women friends.

MEN ASK: WHAT CAN I DO ABOUT A NUMB PENIS?

Sometimes cycling makes the penis go numb. The cause is usually too many miles riding in a bent-over position. The solution is to vary riding position, spend less time in the handlebar drops, and sit upright more. Sometimes a change in handlebar stem helps: If the stem is raised higher, you'll be more upright. If you use a stem with a shorter reach, you'll also be more upright.

Don't put up with this situation—it can lead to permanent nerve damage.

SENIORS ASK: AM I TOO OLD TO RIDE?

Too old to ride? Never. Cycling for those over sixty-five can be excellent for recreation and health. Competition among riders over fifty, sixty, and seventy in organized racing events can be keen. Many members of my Masters racing club compete in licensed USCF events and the Senior Olympics. One member of my club who's still actively racing, Ernest Marinoni, is ninety-one years old!

I'M A SENIOR AND HAVEN'T EXERCISED IN YEARS. SHOULD I SEE A DOCTOR BEFORE STARTING AN EXERCISE PROGRAM?

Certainly. Although physicians don't automatically order a treadmill electrocardiogram on everyone over forty who's beginning an exercise program, as they once did, it's still a good precaution to check with your doc. Start exercise gradually—perhaps only 10 to 15 minutes a few times a week, depending upon your past level of activity and age.

CAN RIDING HELP ME LOSE WEIGHT?

Absolutely, for a number of reasons:

1. Riding burns calories. Depending upon the effort you expend, you can burn more than 1,000 calories per hour, although 250 calories is more typical for new riders working moderately hard.

2. When you ride, you are away from the refrigerator, and you tend to have fewer hours available for eating inappropriately.

3. Riding and exercise can help increase your metabolic rate—the amount of calories you use just to keep your body going.

SHOULD I RIDE WITH A COLD OR THE FLU?

In general, if you have a sore throat or runny nose and feel like riding, it's probably okay to do so. If you feel like resting, that's probably a good idea.

If you are sick, try to choose a route that allows you a shortcut home if things don't work out. If you have a fever, think twice before riding. And if you have symptoms below the neck—for example, chest congestion or wheezing—you'd be wise to stay at home.

HOW DO I FIT RIDING INTO A BUSY SCHEDULE?

It's easy, but you've got to be efficient. If you live a short distance from work, consider that cycling is often faster than travel by car, once you consider parking and other factors. Sure, you might need a shower after commuting, but a shower at work or a nearby gym doesn't take any longer than the one you would have had at home.

Consider riding during your lunch hour—use morning and afternoon breaks to eat. Ride with friends or family. You get the riding you want without cutting out time from family or friends. Use a good-quality halogen light to allow you to ride after dark. And consider a home stationary trainer (a device costing about $150), which allows you to mount your bike and ride time-efficiently at home.

WHY DO MY HANDS (FEET) GO NUMB?

Hands usually go numb when pressure on the palm presses on a nerve. Change your hand position frequently—don't get locked into one spot. Wear padded gloves and use padded handlebar tape.

Feet typically go numb on long hard rides—on hills or into the wind—especially in hot weather. The usual cause is continuous pressure on the foot, or foot swelling related to the heat. Take occasional rests, and take off your shoes and wiggle your toes. Loosen your shoe straps a little when you ride.

WHAT CAN I DO ABOUT SADDLE SORES?

Saddle sores are caused by pressure, friction, or infection. To prevent saddle sores: Keep yourself dry and clean. Wear synthetic, padded, clean shorts. Avoid shorts with seams on pressure areas. Don't increase mileage suddenly. Use seats with padding and support. Change out of those damp shorts as soon as your ride is finished.

To treat saddle sores: Follow the prevention suggestions above, cut back your mileage, and have frequent warm baths. Consider Vaseline or another emollient if your problem is related to friction.

HOW DO I DEAL WITH THE WEATHER?

When it's hot and humid, you need to drink frequently. Wear light-colored clothing, use sunscreen, and reduce the intensity of your riding.

When it's cold, wear layers, including a top layer that provides protection from the wind. A variety of cycling-specific cold-weather gear is available, from long-fingered gloves and long-sleeved jerseys and tights to insulated cycling shoes, helmet liners, and face masks. If it's really miserable outside, consider using your indoor stationary trainer instead.

CAN CYCLING CHANGE MY LIFE?

It can, in many ways. I'm enthusiastic about cycling, whether I am commuting, taking family rides, touring for the day or for weeks at a time, mountain biking, racing, or even riding a stationary trainer in my garage. Whatever kind of riding you do, you may find you are feeling and looking better before long, and who knows: maybe you'll even be a better person. Give it a try, and as Tinker said in the Foreword, if you see me on the road, don't forget to wave.

FOR MORE INFORMATION

BICYCLING BOOKS

Beginning Bicycle Racing
Matheny, Fred. Brattleboro, VT: Velo-news, 1987.
Getting started, training methods, planning.

Bicycle Maintenance & Repair
Bicycling Magazine. Emmaus, PA: Rodale Press, 1990.
A good, general bicycle repair manual.

Bicycle Road Racing
Borysewicz, Edward. Brattleboro, VT: Vitesse Press, 1985.
Excellent though dated overview of road training and racing.

The Bicycle Wheel
Brandt, Jobst. Menlo Park, CA: Avocet, 1981.
Good information even if you don't build your own wheels.

Bicycling Magazine's Cycling for Women
Bicycling Magazine. Emmaus, PA: Rodale Press, 1989.
Good coverage of women's cycling issues.

Bicycling Medicine: Health, Fitness & Injury Explained
Baker, Arnie. New York: Simon & Schuster, 1998.
Cycling nutrition, health, fitness, and injury explained for riders and racers of all levels.

Bike Book
The Diagram Group. Glasgow: HarperCollins, 1994.
Copiously illustrated pocket book of basic bicycling information.

Complete Book of Bicycling
LeMond, Greg. New York: G.P. Putnam's Sons, 1987.
Basic training and tactics, interesting anecdotes.

Cuthbertson's All-in-One Bike Repair Manual
> Cuthbertson, Tom. Berkeley, CA: Ten Speed Press, 1996.
> A good general bicycle repair manual.

Cycling Health and Physiology
> Burke, Edmund. Brattleboro, VT: Vitesse Press, 1992.
> Physiology, nutrition, and training.

Dirt
> Howard, John. New York: The Lyons Press, 1997.
> An overview and philosophy of mountain biking.

Effective Cycling
> Forester, John. Cambridge, MA: MIT Press, 1994.
> Bicycle advocacy: the bicyclist in traffic and society. Bicycle mainte-
> nance.

The Essential Touring Cyclist
> Lovett, Richard. Camden, ME: Ragged Mountain Press, 1994.
> A complete course for the bicycle traveler.

Fit & Fast
> Roy, Karen, and Thurlow Rogers. Brattleboro, VT: Vitesse, 1989.
> Training to be a better cyclist.

Fitness Cycling
> Carmichael, Chris, and Edmund Burke. Champaign, IL: Human
> Kinetics, 1994.
> Basic training and programs for all levels.

Hearts of Lions
> Nye, Peter. New York: W. W. Norton, 1988.
> The story of American cycling heroes and racing.

High-Tech Cycling
> Burke, Edmund. Champaign, IL: Human Kinetics, 1996.
> Biomechanical, technical, and physiologic advances in cycling.

The Mountain Bike Repair Handbook
> Coello, Dennis. New York: Lyons & Burford, 1990.
> A good mountain bicycle repair manual.

The New Complete Mountain Biker
>   Coello, Dennis. New York: Lyons & Burford, 1996.
>   A very good overview of mountain biking.

Richard's Bicycle Repair Manual
>   Ballantine, Richard, and Richard Grant. New York: Dorling Kinder-
>   sley, Inc., 1994.
>   A good, general bicycle repair manual.

Science of Cycling
>   Burke, Edmund. Champaign, IL: Human Kinetics, 1986.
>   Good information on the scientific aspects of cycling.

Serious Cycling
>   Burke, Edmund. Champaign, IL: Human Kinetics, 1995.
>   Cycling training and performance.

Smart Cycling: Training & Racing for Riders of All Levels
>   Baker, Arnie. New York: Simon and Schuster, 1997.
>   Successful training and racing for riders of all levels. The parent
>   book of the training manual of USA Cycling and United States
>   Cycling Federation.

Solo Cycling
>   Matheny, Fred. Brattleboro, VT: Velo-news, 1986.
>   Good hints for time trialing, although now dated.

Training for Cycling
>   Phinney, Davis, and Connie Carpenter. New York: Perigee, 1992.
>   Training and tactics in racing.

Weight Training for Cyclists
>   Matheny, Fred, and Stephen Grabe. Brattleboro, VT: Velo-news,
>   1986.
>   Photos and information about weight training for racers.

The Woman Cyclist
>   Mariolle, Elaine, and Michael Shermer. Chicago: Contemporary
>   Books, 1988.

APPENDIX A

Bicycling from the woman's perspective, with a section on this winning author's Race Across AMerica.

BOOKS WITH SECTIONS
RELEVANT TO BICYCLING

Beyond Training
Williams, Melvin H. Champaign, IL: Leisure Press, 1989.
Legal and illegal enhancement.

Eating for Endurance
Coleman, Ellen. Palo Alto, CA: Bull Publishing Company, 1997.
Excellent book on sport nutrition.

Getting Stronger
Pearl, Bill. Bolinas, CA: Shelter Publications, 1986.
Weight lifting. Has a bicycling section.

The Heart Rate Monitor Book
Edwards, Sally. Port Washington, NY: Polar CIC, 1992.
Basics of heart-rate monitoring.

Serious Training for Serious Athletes
Sleamaker, Rob. Champaign, IL: Leisure Press, 1989.
Framework and philosophy of periodized training.

Stretching
Anderson, Bob. Bolinas, CA: Shelter Publications, 1980.
A classic book on stretching.

Training Lactate Pulse
Janssen, Peter G.J.M. Oulu, Finland: Polar Electro Oy, 1987.
Good concepts in heart-rate training.

CYCLING PERIODICALS

Bicycle Guide
6420 Wilshire Blvd., Los Angeles, CA 90048.
General interest.

Bicycle USA
190 W. Ostend St., Suite 120, Baltimore, MD 21230.
League of American Wheelmen membership magazine.

Bicycling
33 E. Minor St., Emmaus, PA 18098.
General interest.

Cycling USA
1 Olympic Plaza, Colorado Springs, CO 80909.
United States Cycling Federation membership magazine.

Mountain Bike
33 E. Minor St., Emmaus, PA 18098.
Mountain bike news; features on bikes and equipment.

Mountain Bike Action
25233 Anza Dr., Valencia, CA 91355.
Mountain bike news; features on bikes and equipment.

Performance Conditioning for Cycling
POB 6819, Lincoln, NE 68506.
Newsletter dedicated to improving the cyclist.

VeloNews
1830 N. 55th, Boulder, CO 80301.
Racing newspaper; training and equipment articles.

CYCLING ORGANIZATIONS

Cycling USA—United States Cycling Federation
One Olympic Plaza, Colorado Springs, CO 80909.
Telephone (719) 578-4581.
The national governing body of amateur road and track racing.

International Human Powered Vehicle Association
POB 51255, Indianapolis, IN 46251.
Telephone (317) 876-9478.
Promotes innovation of human-powered transport on the land, water, and in the air.

International Mountain Biking Association
POB 412043, Los Angeles, CA 90041.

Telephone (818) 792-8830.

Promotes safe and responsible use of mountain bikes.

League of American Bicyclists
190 West Ostend St., Suite 120, Baltimore, MD 21230.

Telephone (301) 539-3399.

Promotes safe and enjoyable cycling.

National Off-Road Bicycling Association (NORBA)
One Olympic Plaza, Colorado Springs, CO 80909.

Telephone (719) 578-4596.

The national governing body of mountain bike racing.

Recumbent Bicycle Club of America
POB 58755, Renton, WA 98058.

Promotes recumbent cycling.

Tandem Club of America
POB 2176, Los Gatos, CA 95031.

Promotes tandem rallies.

Unicycling Society of America
Box 405234, Redford, MI 48240.

Promotes one-wheeled cycles.

phl.bicycles
Bicycles, bike trails, recreation, and transportation.

rec.bicycles.marketplace
Buying, selling, and reviewing items for cycling.

rec.bicycles.misc
General discussion of bicycling.

rec.bicycles.off-road
All aspects of off-road bicycling.

rec.bicycles.racing
Bicycle racing techniques, rules, and results.

rec.bicycles.rides
Discussions of tours and training or commuting routes.

rec.bicycles.soc
Societal issues of bicycling.

rec.bicycles.tech
Cycling product design, construction, and maintenance.

MONTHLY TRAINING LOG

Date	Distance	Intensity	Location	Group
1				
2				
3				
4				
5				
6				
7				
8				
9				
10				
11				
12				
13				
14				
15				
16				
17				
18				
19				
20				
21				
22				
23				
24				
25				
26				
27				
28				
29				
30				
31				
Total				

For more information about how to keep a training log, see *Keeping a Training Diary* in chapter 6.

MONTHLY TRAINING LOG

Date	Notes	Pulse	Weight
1			
2			
3			
4			
5			
6			
7			
8			
9			
10			
11			
12			
13			
14			
15			
16			
17			
18			
19			
20			
21			
22			
23			
24			
25			
26			
27			
28			
29			
30			
31			
Total			

INDEX

INDEX